Sunderland College

Washington Learning Centre

This book is due for return on or before the last date shown below
Please be aware that sanctions are applied for overdue items
Renew online via Moodle
Renew by phone: call 5116612

Author_ Chapman. S _____

Class __ 401 ____ Location Code ___ EL _____

21 DAY LOAN

PERSPECTIVES ON THE ENGLISH LANGUAGE
Series Editor: Lesley Jeffries

Siobhan Chapman   Thinking About Language: Theories of English
Urszula Clark   Studying Language: English in Action
Lesley Jeffries   Discovering Language: The Structure of Modern English

Perspectives on the English Language Series
Series Standing Order
ISBN 0-333-96146-3 hardback
ISBN 0-333-96147-1 paperback
(outside North America only)

You can receive future titles in this series as they are published by placing a standing order. Please contact your bookseller or, in the case of difficulty, write to us at the address below with your name and address, the title of the series and one of the ISBNs quoted above.

Customer Services Department, Macmillan Distribution Ltd,
Houndmills, Basingstoke, Hampshire RG21 6XS, England

Thinking About Language

Theories of English

Siobhan Chapman

First published 2006 by
PALGRAVE MACMILLAN
Houndmills, Basingstoke, Hampshire RG21 6XS and
175 Fifth Avenue, New York, N.Y. 10010
Companies and representatives throughout the world

PALGRAVE MACMILLAN is the global academic imprint of the Palgrave
Macmillan division of St. Martin's Press, LLC and of Palgrave Macmillan Ltd.
Macmillan® is a registered trademark in the United States, United Kingdom
and other countries. Palgrave is a registered trademark in the European
Union and other countries.

ISBN-13: 978–1–4039–2202–1   hardback
ISBN-10: 1–4039–2202–0   hardback
ISBN-13: 978–1–4039–203–8   paperback
ISBN-10: 1–4039–2203–9   paperback

A catalogue record for this book is available from the British Library.

A catalog record for this book is available from the Library of Congress.

Transferred to Digital Printing 2011

Contents

Series Preface

This series has been a twinkle in my eye for a number of years. I am delighted to be able to launch it with the three 'core' books, *Discovering Language*, *Studying Language* and *Thinking About Language*, which together make a broad introduction to language study in general and the study of English in particular. An explanation of why I felt these books were needed is probably useful here, and it will also serve as an explanation of the series as a whole.

The first thing to note is that English language study is growing in Britain and elsewhere, to some extent at the expense of general linguistics. As a linguistics graduate myself I both regret this and also celebrate the numbers of students wanting to study English language. These students may be studying English language as part of a more general degree course, or as a single subject. All such students need tools of analysis. They need to be able to say what is going on in a text, whether that be a literary or non-literary text, spoken or written. *Discovering Language: The Structure of Modern English* aims to provide just these tools at the level required by undergraduates and their teachers.

Whilst there are many other introductory books on the market, and some of them are very good in different ways, none of them does exactly what *I* want as a teacher of English language undergraduates. I want to be able to teach them the tools of analysis and gain expertise in using them separately from the question of where they come from and whether the theory behind them is consistent or eclectic. We have therefore separated out the contextual and theoretical issues, making sure that all the basic tools are in one volume, *Discovering Language: The Structure of Modern English*, while the issues of context are collected together in *Studying Language: English in Action*, and the basic theories of language which inform all of these approaches are discussed in *Thinking About Language: Theories of English*.

The aim of the second volume, then, *Studying Language: English in Action*, is to put into practice some of the analytical techniques learnt in *Discovering Language*, and to add to these skills by learning about the techniques and problems of studying real language data, either spoken or written, from different points of view, whether social, geographical or even historical. The third book, *Thinking About Language: Theories of English*, enables the student to take a step back from the detail of description and research in order to consider what the underlying views of human language may be. It is likely that students will use these three books at different points in their studies, depending on the kind of course they are taking and the uses their tutors wish to make of them.

The first three books in the series have a logical relationship (description, research and theory), but they can be used in flexible and inventive ways by tutors who find that the individual books do not fit exactly into the modules or course structures they are working to. The series will be developed from here with a 'second wave' of higher-level textbooks, each of which will cover the kind of topic that might be introduced in final-year optional modules or on Masters' courses. These books are currently being commissioned, and the list is not final, but we hope to have titles on English Pragmatics, Conversation Analysis, Critical Discourse Analysis, Literary Stylistics and History of English. They will build upon the core texts by emphasising the three strands of these books: descriptive tools, underlying theories and the methodological issues relating to each topic. They will be written by scholars at the cutting edge of research, and will include both an overview and the latest developments in the field concerned.

LESLEY JEFFRIES

Acknowledgements

I would like to thank Lesley Jeffries, editor of this series, for giving me the opportunity to write this book and for providing support and encouragement throughout the process of writing it. Thanks also to Lesley and to Urszula Clark who, as authors of the other two companion books in the series, have remained enthusiastic and cheerful throughout the project of producing the three books.

I would also like to thank Kate Wallis and her team at Palgrave Macmillan for their unwavering faith in the project and for seeing it through to completion with efficiency and great patience.

The School of English at the University of Liverpool afforded me some much appreciated teaching remission while I was writing this book.

SIOBHAN CHAPMAN

Introduction

The principal aims of this book are to introduce some of the ways in which theory has affected what people have said about language in the past and why they have said it, and to investigate the continued effect of theory on how linguists think about language today. It is not intended as an introduction to particular theories in the individual branches of linguistics. For example it does not have much to say about different theories that have been developed in phonology or in syntax. Still less is it intended to serve as an introduction to linguistic theory as a particular area or specialist subject within general linguistics. Indeed, one of the central tenets of this book could be summarized as 'theory is everywhere'; every approach to the study of language involves some theoretical assumptions or commitments. It is an intention of this book to encourage readers of linguistics always to keep this in mind and to become adept at spotting these assumptions and commitments and recognising their significance.

In relation to the companion books in this series, this book encourages the reader to step back from specific linguistic analyses and consider the broader questions underlying the study of language. These include issues such as what the main purpose of language is, how language operates when we communicate with each other, and indeed what constitutes the appropriate subject matter of linguistics. However language theory also has a role to play in specific linguistic analyses. Linguistic analysis is of course a valuable activity in its own right and a useful source of information about language. But it is always underpinned by some prior decisions about language, and an awareness of these decisions is very useful in understanding and interpreting the findings of the analysis.

If there is a single most important argument in this book it is this: linguists say the things that they do say about language because of assumptions they have made about how best to study it. These assumptions are sometimes made explicit in linguistic writing, perhaps even forming the central topic of an article or book. Sometimes they remain implicit. In either case the assumptions will affect factors such as what linguists choose to investigate, how they go about investigating it, and how they analyse and interpret their findings. A full understanding of writings from across the range of fields and topics in linguistics therefore depends on at least a basic familiarity with these assumptions, together with a sensitivity to what motivates them and what their implications are. This book touches on a wide range of approaches and schools of thought in linguistics. But the emphasis is always on highlighting the relevant assumptions. For this reason the approaches and schools of thought are not explored in much detail. For instance the book does not include full introductions to Chomskyan, functional or behaviourist linguistics. Rather it concentrates on how each of these schools of thought relates to the range of different assumptions that underpin the study of language in general. It encourages readers to find out more about the approaches for themselves, while keeping the significance of the different assumptions in mind.

Part I offers an overview of some of the big issues in language theory. For instance it considers what counts as appropriate data for different types of language study, what types of theory there are, and the close links between types of data and types of theory. It also demonstrates how thinkers about language have come up with a strikingly wide range of answers to the question 'What is language?', and how these different answers have had far-reaching consequences for how linguists have looked at language and the conclusions they have drawn. The chapters in Part I contain quite a large number of quotations from both primary sources and introductory textbooks. These quotations serve two purposes. They offer readers short examples of how to read linguistics with an eye to theoretical commitments, and of how these commitments tend to be made overt, or be hidden, in texts. They also point readers to a range of primary and secondary sources where they can find out much more about the areas touched on here. Each chapter concludes with a 'Further reading' section that outlines where the relevant topics and issues are taken up or discussed in more detail in the two companion books in this series, as well as other works on the topics in question.

A large proportion of Part I is dedicated to three different answers to the question 'What is language?' These answers are paraphrased as 'Language is a type of behaviour', 'Language is a state of mind' and 'Language is communication'. In each case, some examples of thinkers whose ideas have fallen into these broad categories are discussed. The intention is not to offer a comprehensive historical overview of the relevant answer, but to focus on some of the forms in which it has appeared in language study and to enable readers to identify and evaluate other occurrences of it in future reading. In Chapter 2, the section concerned with the second of these answers (Section 2.2) is the only one to concentrate exclusively on the work of one thinker: Noam Chomsky. This is not intended to give Chomsky's ideas undue weight in the discussion of theory of language. Chomsky is just one thinker, although arguably the most prominent, in a 'mentalist' tradition that has a long history. Readers can find out more about this tradition by following up the references in Chomsky's own work. Furthermore the concentration on Chomsky reflects the huge impact that his reinterpretation of mentalism has had on linguistics. Much recent work has defined itself in relation to his ideas. Anyone who reads widely in linguistics will come across responses to Chomsky, and therefore it is important to be familiar with what Chomsky has said and why. The subsequent section is concerned with understandings of language as communication, and it considers some of the more hostile responses to Chomsky. In fact the three sections in Chapter 2 are designed in part to show that the Chomskyan framework is only one way of looking at language. In other words, linguistic theory does not equate to Chomskyan theory, as has sometimes been assumed in recent linguistics, including in some linguistics textbooks.

The chapters in Part II are more narrowly focused and highly structured than those in Part I. Each is concerned with a particular question about language, and the various sections of each chapter outline some of the different answers that have been proposed. With the exception of the more discursive final chapter, each chapter includes a brief 'Focus on . . . ' section, which singles out the ideas of one theorist or one school of thought for consideration. These are ideas that have had a particular influence on how linguists have thought about the relevant question in language study.

The questions raised in Part II are all central to specialist linguistics, but they are also intended to have more everyday appeal: to be the types of issue that ordinary people speculate about when they think about language. Each chapter emphasises the different attitudes towards language, and sometimes the different attitudes towards theory and data, that are apparent in all the possible answers to the question under consideration. Whenever relevant, attention is drawn to the links between these ideas and the approaches to language discussed in Part I.

A recurrent theme in all the chapters in Part II is that there is generally no single answer to any of the most intriguing questions about language that is self-evidently true. Agreement or even compromise is unlikely ever to be reached because of the widely different backgrounds from which and assumptions with which theorists have approached these questions. Rather than being a weak spot in linguistics, or suggesting a series of dead ends in linguistic inquiry, this is something to be celebrated. It demonstrates that there are no easy answers in language study, and it highlights the importance of paying proper attention to the theoretical commitments that always underpin it.

As noted above, and with the exception of the final chapter, each chapter concludes with a 'Further reading' section that provides links to topics covered in this book's companion volumes and lists the more accessible of the primary sources discussed in each chapter, as well as relevant introductions and other secondary sources. Each chapter in Part II could therefore form the basis of research towards a presentation, essay or project. As well as offering a starting point for such research, the individual chapters outline a range of ideas that could be investigated in more detail and could be either defended or challenged.

Introducing
Language Theory

Theory in Language Study

This book is about the ways in which theory can help us to think about language. It is about how theory can get us started in looking for answers to the significant and interesting questions that thinking about language raises. It is important to remember that we are not doing something different or unusual when we use theory in this way. It does not make much sense to think about theoretical approaches to language as forming a specialist branch of linguistics, distinct from normal or non-theoretical linguistics. In fact, when it comes to doing linguistics it is almost impossible to avoid theory of one sort or another. As soon as linguists make an assumption about language, or choose a method by which to investigate it, there is a theoretical aspect to what they are doing. Later in Part I we will look at three different assumptions about language, and consider the effects these have had on how people have studied language and what conclusions about it they have drawn.

The effects of assumptions about language are not restricted to big theories of language, or to the differences between the major schools of thought in linguistics. Even apparently straightforward descriptions of language, including those discussed in the other companion books in this series, are based on theoretical commitments. For instance *Discovering Language* (Jeffries, 2006) discusses the elements that make up the phrases, clauses and sentences of English. This is not the only possible way of describing a language; it is based on some ideas that linguists have developed, and that they have found useful, to show order and pattern in what might otherwise seem chaotic and random. *Studying Language* (Clark, 2006) includes practical information on how to record and transcribe tape recordings. This too draws on some assumptions: in particular the assumption that examples of 'real life' language use is an important source of evidence in linguistics. This is an interesting idea, but it is far from being self-evidently true. We will see soon that many linguists

7

would simply not agree with it. In general, differences in opinion about how to go about doing linguistics, or arguments about methodology, tend to mask much bigger underlying differences. They generally result from differences over the question of what the subject matter of linguistics actually is.

So linguists start out with some assumptions about language, and these influence how they decide to investigate it and may well have an effect on what conclusions they reach. Sometimes these assumptions are made clear at the start of a book or article, but sometimes it takes a bit of effort to work out what they are. It is a good idea to get into the habit of spotting such assumptions in whatever you are reading. This will make it easier to assess the significance of the argument and the conclusions, and also help you to compare different pieces of work that have drawn on different assumptions. As a first example, here is the very beginning of *Word and Object*, a collection of essays by the American philosopher W. V. O. Quine:

> Language is a social art. In acquiring it we have to depend entirely on intersubjectively available cues as to what to say and when. Hence there is no justification for collating linguistic meanings, unless in terms of men's dispositions to respond overtly to socially observable stimulations (Quine, 1960, p. ix).

Quine is well known for his belief that language exists only as a form of behaviour: that in studying language we must look only at what people do on particular occasions. We will look at this belief and its implications in Chapter 2, but we can see his position set out clearly and explicitly in these opening lines. Quine defines language entirely in terms of social interaction. It is an art, or a skill that people employ when interacting with each other. Learning it involves picking up cues, or indications as to how to employ this skill. Quine rules out the possibility of discussing meaning in language ('collating linguistic meanings') in any way other than in relation to how people behave in certain situations. In all cases, what linguists are describing must be available for observation. Any utterance they discuss must be made overtly, and the relevant context must be observable. Quine goes on to discuss language in complex and intricate ways in *Word and Object*, but everything he says about it is based on these specific premises.

Compare Quine's opening remarks with those of another important thinker about language. Noam Chomsky has very different views from Quine on what language is, and we will consider these views in more detail in Chapters 2 and 9. Very briefly, Chomsky sees language as a formal system; a language is a set of grammatical rules that exist in people's minds and is capable of producing all the possible sentences. When we study language we have to be careful not to be distracted by all sorts of social and personal factors that might influence how people speak but are nothing to do with that set of grammatical rules. If we look at just the first two sentences of Chomsky's first book, *Syntactic Structures*, we can identify some of these ideas:

> Syntax is the study of the principles and processes by which sentences are constructed in particular languages. Syntactic investigation of a given language has as its goal the construction of a grammar that can be viewed as a device of some sort for producing the sentences of the language under analysis (Chomsky, 1957, p. 11).

Chomsky tells us that there are 'principles and processes' that put together the sentences of a language, and that the business of syntax, which for Chomsky is the central part of linguistics, is to compile a list of these principles and processes, or a grammar of the language. However there are other views in this short extract that are not made so obvious but are equally important to understanding the ideas about language that are being put forward. Chomsky assumes that a language is essentially made up of sentences and that these sentences can be studied in their own right. This is an interesting point of view, but it is far from being obviously true and, as we will see, many linguists would disagree with it. Chomsky is further assuming that sentences exist independently of any situation or occasion of use. There is simply no mention of society or contexts, or even of the people who use a language. This is all very different from Quine's bold declaration that language exists only insofar as it used in society.

One way of explaining this is to say that Chomsky's ideas are 'reductionist'. That is, he tackles an apparently unmanageable task, that of explaining everything about human language, by concentrating only on one aspect of the problem. He reduces the task to a discussion of simpler and therefore potentially more manageable features. For Chomsky, explaining language does not involve taking on the full range of factors that might affect how people speak. It is the much more restricted, although still immensely complex, task of describing the grammatical rules that produce sentences. In order to recognise this belief, you have to read his words carefully and think about what is left unsaid as well as what is made explicit.

Many linguists have criticised Chomsky for his reductionism, and we will look at some of their arguments in more detail later in Part I. One branch of linguistics that has taken a broader approach, arguing that explaining language is not just about grammar, is sociolinguistics. Linguists in this branch claim that any explanation of language has to take account of the social situations in which language occurs and the social factors that affect how speakers relate to each other. In sociolinguistics too we can find some assumptions that influence the process and outcomes of the study of language. In order to understand this we will consider Bernard Spolsky's *Sociolinguistics* (1998). This is a very different type of book, with a different purpose, from Chomsky's *Syntactic Structures*. It is a textbook, designed to summarise and explain other people's work, rather than to put forward a new set of ideas. And of course it is concerned with the ideas of sociolinguistics rather than those of syntactic theory. In fact, in the opening pages of his book Spolsky makes a point of drawing a distinction between Chomsky's assumptions about language and those of sociolinguistics:

> Sociolinguistics is the field that studies the relation between language and society, between the users of language and the social structures in which the users of language live. It is a field of study that assumes that human society is made up of many related patterns and behaviours, some of which are linguistic (Spolsky, 1998, p. 3).

Here too there are both explicit and less obvious claims about language and linguistics. Spolsky offers a clear account of the main ideas in sociolinguistics. Speakers of languages live in societies, so in order fully to understand language linguists must take into account the structures of society. Language is a form of behaviour, and as such is comparable with a number of other forms of behaviour. But the assumptions do not end there, and in fact we can detect some reductionism even in this statement of the aims of sociolinguistics. In order to do sociolinguistics at all it is necessary to accept that language is in some way a distinct, identifiable type of behaviour, one that can be isolated from all other forms of behaviour. Otherwise sociolinguists would not be able to say that some types of behaviour are linguistic and others are not. Furthermore the very idea that people can be described as 'users of language' implies that language exists separately from its users or from any instance of linguistic behaviour. These may well seem like reasonable assumptions to make, but again they are far from accepted by everyone. Above all it is important to remember that they are assumptions rather than obvious facts, and that the way that sociolinguists work and the conclusions they draw may well be influenced by them.

Even those approaches to language study that are sometimes said to be theory-free, or at least based entirely on observable facts rather than speculation, are necessarily involved in some founding assumptions about language and some reductions. Corpus linguistics is a case in point. We will consider this approach to language study in Chapter 2. It involves looking at large quantities of written or spoken language, recorded in electronic form on computers, in order to find out about various features of the language under investigation. Sticking for the time being with opening lines, here is the one from a textbook on corpus linguistics: 'Corpus linguistics is perhaps best described for the moment in simple terms as the study of language based on examples of "real life" language use' (McEnery and Wilson, 1996, p. 1). This is a clear and apparently straight-forward definition, but it is not free from assumptions and reductions. First of all there is the reference to 'real life' examples. This suggests that text recorded on a computer some time after the original event of writing or speaking is authentic, or true to life. It may well be a necessary assumption to make for corpus linguistics to get off the ground, or for corpus linguists to be able to say anything interesting about language. But it is not obviously or uncontroversially true. It might be possible to claim that once corpus linguists take an example away from the context in which it was originally produced they are altering it in significant ways. In effect they are relying on the assumption that one can extract language from a situation, or reduce a complex action to a purely linguistic element, and still be left with something authentic to study. There are further assumptions implicit in the phrase 'language use', which we have already considered in relation to sociolinguistics. Again the authors of this textbook are assuming that language has the potential to be 'used' in different circumstances, hence that it in some sense exists independently of those individual instances of use.

It may well be the case that linguistics is always, necessarily, reductive; it is just the choice of specific reductions, or perhaps the scale of reductionism, that varies. In order for language study to be possible at all, it is necessary to abstract away from the coincidental features of language use and concentrate on what is essential to language itself. This leaves open the question of which features are coincidental and which are essential, and language theorists have made widely different decisions on this issue.

In the next chapter we will look at three different theoretical approaches to the study of language, and consider what has motivated each of them and what implications they have. Each of these approaches is based on a particular view of what linguists study. This might at first glance seem like a very odd statement; surely what linguists study is language? But as we will see, the question of what language is, or how we can best define the subject matter of linguistics, is far from being a straightforward matter. Each of the three approaches suggests a specific answer to the question 'What is language?'

This question is different from another important question that looks deceptively similar, namely 'What is *a* language?' Attempting to answer this second question makes linguists think about different possible ways of defining any particular language such as English, Russian or Urdu. It means deciding what makes the difference between saying that two people speak different languages and saying that they speak different dialects of the same language. And it involves explaining why we might want to say that although a language changes over time it remains fundamentally the same language. But many linguists see the question 'What is language?' as a more fundamental problem, and claim that it is necessary to make some decisions about this before going on to any of the more specific issues.

Before we turn to some of the answers that have been suggested to this question, it is worth thinking about the general issue of why they are important in the first place, or of why theory is necessary or even appropriate in the study of language. It is not hard to imagine the arguments that people who want to oppose theory in language study might put. They might argue that language is a natural phenomenon, and that it is therefore not appropriate to try to explain it by means of some abstract, artificial theory. They might point out that language is far more complex than any neat theoretical description could explain, because it is decided on a day-to-day or even minute-to-minute basis by the needs and wishes of individual speakers who use it in everyday situations. Or they might complain that you can prove any theory you care to come up with, so long as you are prepared to select your examples carefully to match your theory. If we think about each of these arguments in turn we will find some interesting things to say in reply to the critics of theory, and in the process discover something about the importance of theory in language study.

We can answer the first argument without having to deny that language is a natural phenomenon. Indeed the subject matter of linguistics is often described as being 'natural language' to distinguish it from invented, artificial languages such as those used in logic and in computing. Knowing and using a language seems to be a natural part of what it is to be a human being, and human languages are not invented or designed. But to agree that something is a natural phenomenon is not the same as admitting that it should not be explained by a theory. Indeed many theories in other areas of study suggest explanations of natural phenomena. The theory of evolution offers an account of the origin of the vast variety of life forms on the planet, and an explanation of the natural fact that species apparently change over time. The theory of gravity explains why objects fall to the ground when dropped, how planets orbit and why we do not fall off the Earth. And the theory of molecular structure gives us a way of discussing the actions and interactions of the different substances around us. In each case the theoretical explanation does not imply that the subject matter under investigation must also be theoretical or artificial. The point of the theory is to say more than could be said by a simple description of the relevant facts, and in each case the theory has been viewed as successful because it has had something interesting to say about those facts. Of course these three examples are all taken from the physical sciences: from biology, physics and chemistry respectively. Some linguists claim that linguistics too is a science, and that linguistic theory explains the phenomena of language just as, say, physical theory explains the phenomena of matter, energy and time. Not everyone agrees that linguistics can be classified quite so straightforwardly as a science, but linguists are generally happy to compare linguistic theories to scientific theories, and to see scientific theories as providing a good basis for what a theory should be like. As we will see in the rest of Part I, linguists are not always in agreement about what makes a theory truly scientific.

We can also use this relationship between linguistics and scientific theories in our response to the second criticism. In the sciences the complexity of a subject matter is no reason to abandon the search for a theory to explain it. On the contrary, it is often precisely because a natural phenomenon appears to be extremely complex that scientists look for a theoretical explanation. It is not that they want to 'explain away' the apparent complexity, or to pretend that things are much neater and more straightforward than they really are in order to make life easier. Rather scientists realise that it is only by focusing on certain features of a situation that they can say something constructive and systematic about what is going on. A physicist describing the path of a leaf falling from a tree could not possibly hope to give an exact description of all the relevant factors, including air resistance and wind direction, and the interaction of the shape and structure of the leaf with these. But it is still worth using the theory of gravity to explain something about the movement of the leaf, rather than just giving up because explaining everything is too complicated. A similar argument can be used in relation to language study. What any individual says at any particular moment might well be decided by a hugely complex set of factors, including the personality of the speaker, what mood he or she is in, what – if anything – has been said immediately before. It would be unrealistic to expect to be able to devise a theory that took all these different factors into consideration. It would also be undesirable; a theory that managed to account for everything would necessarily be so broad and so general that it would end up telling us nothing very interesting at all. But it is still possible to say something about the language the speaker is using, even if this forms only one part of the complex situation that holds when the language is used.

The final criticism suggested above, the one about the possibility of proving just about any theory by choosing your examples, is repeated quite frequently and is potentially a serious one. It would indeed be inappropriate to make grand claims for the success of a theory that explained a small selection of examples but could not be applied beyond that limited set. But in fact any linguistic theory that is treated as interesting or significant must be able to cope with examples beyond those it was initially designed to explain. We will consider in Section 1.2 how a theory might be tested in relation to those further examples, and what would determine whether it could cope with them successfully.

As we have seen, the study of language must necessarily include some element of theory, so it can be misleading to talk about theoretical approaches to language as though they were in some way specialised or unusual. As soon as linguists start describing something as complex as language, they have to make decisions about what sort of things it contains, and about which features are similar and which are different. These decisions are imposed on the language rather than just being there in the evidence. The linguists are using some sort of theory of language. However theory in language study also makes it possible to go beyond these types of description to consider more general questions about language, and it is with these that we will mainly be concerned in this book.

When it comes to these more general questions, theory is usually a much more central and prominent part of the study. This is not to say that the theory takes over, or becomes the main focus of study in its own right. But it does mean that the theory allows us to focus on some of the features of language that we cannot so obviously observe and describe. It allows us to consider, for instance, the nature of the relationship between words and the things in the world they describe, or between language and thought. This is part explains why the issue of the appropriate type of evidence, or of what linguists should study, is so significant. If we want to know what speech sounds there are in a certain language, or whether subjects come before verbs or the other way round, we can collect some examples and examine them to find an answer. But there is no obvious evidence that we can collect and examine in search of an answer to the bigger questions. In these cases, theory allows us to go beyond a list of examples to consider, for instance, what makes language unique, and how we use it to make sense of the world around us and relate to each other.

1.1 Types of data

We have seen that different approaches to linguistics can start from different answers to the question 'What is language?' To put this another way, they start from different points of view about the nature of the data in linguistics. 'Data' is the name given to the set of information, or observable facts, in any particular area of study. Strictly speaking any one such piece of information is called a datum, and data is the plural of this word, describing several separate pieces of information, or even the full set of all relevant pieces of information. Nowadays, however, the word data tends to be treated grammatically as though it were singular. You will come across sentences such as 'my data is selected from a range of different sources' at least as frequently as the more strictly correct 'My data are selected from a range of different sources'. To fit in with this practice we will use 'data' as a singular noun.

What counts as relevant data of course varies from subject to subject. The data for an investigation in geography, for instance, might be information about the population in different cities or the rainfall in different countries. Relevant data in economics might include information about prices, incomes and savings. So there is no doubt that the data for linguistic study comes from language, but we are still left with the question of what type of data language has to offer, or of what language actually consists of. When we were considering the ways in which theories become involved whenever we think about language, we compared Noam Chomsky's ideas about what linguists should study with those put forward by sociolinguists. These two sets of ideas include very different takes on what language is, and as a direct consequence the two styles of linguistics use different types of data.

Chomsky belongs to what is known as the 'mentalist' tradition in linguistics. We will look at mentalist approaches to linguistics in more detail in Chapter 2, when we consider the view that language is a state of mind. As we will see, the set of grammatical rules that for Chomsky define a language exist in the minds of people who speak that language. Therefore according to Chomsky linguists are studying something about the human mind. Everything they need to know about a language is contained in the mind of someone who speaks that language. So the best way to study a language is to ask speakers questions about what they know, for instance by suggesting various possible sentences and asking them to judge whether these conform to the rules of their grammar. Not only do linguists not need to look elsewhere for their data, it could actually be misleading for them to do so. If they look at examples of people using language, there is a danger that they might end up concentrating on things to do with context or interpersonal relationships that have nothing to do with grammatical rules.

Because the data for mentalist linguistics comes from asking people to think about what they know about a language, or to introspect their own knowledge, it is sometimes described as introspective data. Mentalist linguists argue that it is perfectly acceptable for them to do their own introspection, and to use their own knowledge of the language as their data. Language data can be provided by any speaker of the language. Mentalist linguists do, however, attach particular significance to the notion of a 'native speaker': someone who has learnt the language by growing up with it and acquiring it as a child, rather than learning it later in life. It is only from native speakers that they can be sure of getting reliable data on a particular language. For this reason mentalist linguists studying a language other than their own need to find one or more native speakers of that language to tell them about the language, or to act as their informants.

The picture is rather different in sociolinguistics. Linguists who are interested in the relationship between language and social context necessarily have to find out about how language is used in different contexts. Relying on their own intuitive knowledge, or asking informants what they know about their language, will not be enough because it will not produce any information about how different contexts affect how people speak. Sociolinguists, and those working in any of the other branches of linguistics that study how language is used in social situations, go out and collect their data. Generally this involves recording conversations on tape recorders or video cameras, and often transcribing these recordings into a written version. Sociolinguists also sometimes use questionnaires to gather their data, in the tradition of work in social sciences such as sociology.

Differences between mentalist linguists and those working in traditions such as sociolinguistics sometimes lead to disagreements, and even heated debate, about what is the 'right' type of data to use in linguistics. But ultimately this is not a debate that can be settled. Different types of data are suitable for different types of study. As long as there are different ideas about the answer to the question 'What is language?' there will be linguists working with different types of data. And the wide variety of possible answers to that question is one of the things that make linguistics such a fascinating subject.

1.2   Types of theory

Nearly all present-day linguists are keen to explain what they do as 'descriptive', as distinct from 'prescriptive', linguistics. They want to distance themselves from any notion that they are trying to lay down rules for how people ought to behave when using language, or to label some forms of language as correct and others as incorrect. This is what goes on in prescriptive linguistics, such as that found in some old-fashioned grammar books. A prescriptive linguist might tell you that it is incorrect to end a sentence in English with a preposition: *That is the man about whom I told you* is correct, but *That is the man I told you about* includes a grammatical mistake. A descriptive linguist, on the other hand, will be more interested in observing what speakers of English actually do. They might note that the second version is much more likely to occur in spoken and written English than the first version or comment that it will appear more natural to most native speakers of English. Indeed descriptive linguists believe that the rule about not ending sentences with prepositions is a more or less arbitrary one that has very little to do with English itself but has been imposed on the language by prescriptive linguists because of some facts about Latin grammar.

Prescriptive linguistics is generally now seen as marginal and old-fashioned. However there are some current approaches to linguistics that make claims about how people ought to use language rather than describing how they do use it. For instance feminist linguists and advocates of political correctness argue that the pronouns *he* and *his* ought not to be used as generics in sentences such as *Every student must hand his essay in on time*, because such uses exclude women or present the male as the norm. This might be seen as a form of modern-day prescriptivism, and indeed adherents of political correctness are quite happy to describe it as a justifiably prescriptivist movement.

Theoretical approaches to language generally belong to the descriptive tradition in linguistics. Whatever assumptions about language they start out with, their purpose is to find out something about language as it actually is, not as a purist would like it to be. As we have seen, linguists use theory to say something more about language than they could from just an accumulation of data. However not everyone who uses theory to go beyond the data and consider wider questions uses the same methods. That is, not everyone makes their theory and their data work together in the same way. In order to understand this we need to look a little at how scientists have thought about the function and operation of their theories. This is because ideas about theory that are most closely associated with the natural sciences have also had a significant impact on the ways in which language has been, and still is, studied.

Imagine that you are a scientist interested in finding out about some aspect of the world: say about types of flower. You might well decide to start your study by going out and looking at some flowers and finding out what you can about them. You will probably decide quite quickly that you will need to work with theory to some extent if you are going to get anywhere. Without theory all you can do is accumulate data: perhaps flowers that you have collected, or descriptions of flowers that you have observed. If someone asks you what you have found out so far, all you can do is show them this collection of data. You findings are just as complicated, and just as unstructured, as the data itself.

A good first step might be to try to make some general statements about your data. Perhaps you have collected a number of white daisies, but no daisies of any other colour. Instead of just listing your data (*Here's a white daisy . . . here's a white daisy . . . here's a white daisy*) it would be more useful and interesting to make a general statement, such as *All the daisies I have collected are white*. This is better than the simple list of data but it still does not tell you much about your area of study. It tells you about the particular examples of daisies you happen to have come across, not about daisies in general. Things get a lot more interesting if you try going beyond your immediate data and saying something such as *All daisies are white*. In doing this you are making a general statement about how the world is, based on some specific pieces of evidence. To put it another way, you are making a prediction; you are predicting that if you go on collecting data you will find many more instances of white daisies but no instances of daisies of any other colour.

The method of relating theory and data that we have just been considering is known as the inductive method, or as working by induction. An inductive investigation of any phenomenon starts with, and is driven by, the data. It involves gathering relevant examples of the subject matter under investigation, and then looking closely at this data to discern any general trends or patterns. As well as being a valid scientific method, induction is the method by which we generally make sense of the world around us. In many areas of life we are not constantly surprised by events because we are constantly making predictions about what is likely to happen next. These predictions are produced by generalising from individual pieces of relevant past experience. If we see thick black clouds when we are going out, we are likely to take an umbrella with us. This is not because we know for certain that it will rain, but because we have had a number of past experiences of black clouds being followed by rain. Our past experience gives us a strong enough motive to agree with the statement *Black clouds mean rain*, and certainly a strong enough motive to take an umbrella to avoid getting wet. All this seems no more than common sense. We would not get anywhere in life if we stopped to ponder about the nature and certainty of our knowledge all the time. The prediction that black clouds mean rain is not definite. The many instances of black clouds followed by rain we have experienced in the past do not guarantee that this particular black cloud will be followed by rain on this occasion. But the past connection makes our expectation of rain highly probable, and this is good enough for us.

Some theorists have questioned whether this type of probabilistic knowledge is good enough for science. Take for instance the claim that *The sun will rise in the east tomorrow*. As far as ordinary life is concerned we are nearly certain of the truth of this prediction. There have been so many instances of the sun rising in the east that it seems certain that this will also be the case tomorrow. We have positive knowledge of numerous previous instances of the sun rising in the east, and from these we draw a probabilistic but in practice near-certain prediction. But speaking in strictly scientific terms we do not know that tomorrow the sun will rise in the east. However strong our positive knowledge of past events, it is possible that the sun will not rise at all tomorrow, or will surprise us by rising in the west instead. In a similar although rather less dramatic fashion, however many white daisies we collect our claim that *All daisies are white* remains probabilistic rather than definite. Even a very large number of white daisies does not rule out the possibility that somewhere out there is a red daisy.

There is a further problem for induction as a scientific method, beyond the issue of the probabilistic nature of inductive statements. This problem has to do with the nature of the data that counts as support for an inductive statement, and it takes the form of a philosophical paradox. That is, the nature of induction seems to lead inevitably to a particular conclusion that is bizarre in itself, and contrary to what we expect. This particular paradox was pointed out by Carl Hempel, a mid-twentieth-century philosopher who began to doubt the validity of the inductive method.

Hempel's example was *All ravens are black*, a claim that we might reasonably reach by induction, after observing lots of examples of black ravens and no examples of ravens of any other colour. Hempel pointed out that, logically speaking, the claim that *All ravens are black* is equivalent to the claim that *All non-black things are non-ravens*. That is, if all ravens are black then anything that is not black cannot be a raven; it must be something else. If *All ravens are black* is true then *All non-black things are non-ravens* must also be true. One consequence of this logical equivalence is that if we find some evidence that supports the claim that *All non-black things are non-ravens*, then this piece of evidence must also support the equivalent claim that *All ravens are black*. Our inductive claim is supported every time we see a black raven. But it is also supported every time we see something that is not a raven and is not black. A white horse, a red apple, a purple tree, a blue cow: an observation of any of these things provides evidence in support of the claim that *All ravens are black*. Here is the paradox. It seems utterly bizarre, and contrary to all our expectations of the 'common sense' nature of induction, that a blue cow should count as evidence in support of the claim that *All ravens are black*. But this unacceptable conclusion seems to be a necessary consequence of the nature of induction itself.

Positive knowledge based on generalisations from individual observations was highly valued in the philosophy of science in the middle of the twentieth century, particularly within the school of thought known as logical positivism. In Chapter 4 we will look at the consequences of this approach for claims about meaning in language. As we will see, these claims proved very controversial, and in response to them some wholly different ideas were put forward as to how best to think about language. In the philosophy of science, too, thinkers began to question induction as a method. This was in part because of the paradox about relevant evidence that we have just considered, which seemed to call into question the validity of the inductive method itself. It was also because of worries about how far scientists could get by generalising from particular observations. One person who was particularly associated with the reaction against the inductive method of logical positivism was Karl Popper. The alternative to induction, closely associated with the work of Popper, is nowadays generally known as deduction, or the deductive method of science.

We could summarise the deductive method, in contrast to the inductive method, by saying that it is theory-driven rather than data-driven. The theory is the focus and the starting point, with the data playing a supporting but vital role as a means of testing the theory. Scientists who want to explain some aspect of the natural world deductively start with a general claim, or hypothesis, about how things are. Popper himself was rather vague about where the all-important hypothesis comes from. He seems to have seen it as resulting from inspiration, rather as if the scientist were a creative artist:

> The question how it happens that a new idea occurs to a man – whether it is a musical theme, a dramatic conflict, or a scientific theory – may be of great interest to empirical psychology; but it is irrelevant to the logical analysis of scientific knowledge (Popper, 2002, p. 7).

In reality the beginnings of a hypothesis are unlikely to be completely detached from the data. Some initial observation, or a very small set of data, may suggest a general explanation that is developed into a theory. If this theory explains the initial observations, then so far it is adequate and useful. But to be a successful deductive theory it must do more than that: it must stand up to the test of further data. In the deductive method the data does not function to provide repeated confirmations of the theory. In fact the theory may be such that it cannot be directly supported by any positive data. The theory may be a hypothesis about the underlying, unobservable causes of observable phenomena.

What is important to a deductive hypothesis, indeed what makes it a valid scientific statement, is not that it can be supported by data but rather that it can be falsified. That is, the hypothesis must make specific predictions that can be tested against data and can in principle be proved wrong. This may at first sight seem like a very strange claim to make. To be of any use a theory must be capable of being proved wrong. But for supporters of the deductive method the only theories that can be taken seriously are those for which it is possible to state clearly what would count as a counterexample. The theory tells us something about how the world is, and makes predictions about what we will find in the world as a result. The relevant data is then used to test the validity of these predictions, and therefore of the theory itself. Scientists who use the deductive method are not looking for lots of data to support their theory. They are on the look-out for any one piece of data that will falsify their theory. If we deductively test our claim that *All daisies are white* we are not interested in accumulating instances of white daisies. Rather we are interested in the possibility of discovering a daisy that is not white. A single daisy that is red or blue or yellow will act as a counterexample to the predictions made by our theory, and will falsify it.

When a falsifying counterexample to a theory is identified, scientists have two options. They may decide that the theory is not going to work; the new data includes serious counterexamples, or examples that go completely against what the theory predicts and there is no option but to abandon the theory. Or they may decide that the theory can be retained in basically its original form but that it needs to be modified in some way to explain the new as well as the original data. This leads scientists to refine their theory, and yet more data may cause them to refine it further; the theory is in a constant state of modification and improvement. Importantly, there is no need for an unattainable hope of proving the theory. If scientists collect some new data and it fits the theory, that may boost their confidence in the theory but it can never prove that it is correct; it is always possible that the next bit of data may present problems. What is important is that the theory should be falsifiable. That is, the scientists should know with confidence what sort of data would lead them to acknowledge that there was a problem with the theory, and to modify or abandon it. If it is not possible to imagine any type of data that would falsify the theory, then the theory itself is of no value because it can never be put to the test by means of data. To be described as 'unfalsifiable' is probably the worst possible insult for a deductive theory.

On the face of it, adopting a deductive approach might seem to be a very precarious undertaking. Deductive scientists commit themselves to a theory, based perhaps on little more than a hunch, and then live in the constant expectation that the next piece of data they come across might falsify it. Induction might produce probabilistic statements, but the claims of deduction are always contingent. As Popper forcefully claimed, 'every scientific statement must remain *tentative for ever*' (Popper, 2002, p. 280, emphasis in original). But those who support the deductive method argue that it is only by taking these risks that they are able to say interesting things about the world. Using the inductive method can take you beyond a mere list of the data, but not much beyond it. You can generalise over your observations and make predictions about similar observations in the future. But with the deductive method you can go beyond the evidence immediately available to you and speculate about things for which you have no direct evidence, perhaps things for which no direct evidence is possible. As long as your theory makes definite predictions, and therefore can be falsified, you will be making a valid claim about how the world is.

Deduction may have become established as part of the reaction against the problems of induction, but it did not replace induction and become the only legitimate scientific method. And deduction is not without problems of its own. For instance some people have argued that neither Popper nor anyone else has ever successfully defined what counts as falsification. Popper certainly seemed to imply that any one observation that provided a counterexample to a prediction made by a theory would be enough to falsify that theory. But some thinkers have questioned whether that is really a satisfactory state of affairs; should a whole theory really be modified or disposed of in response to one little piece of data? And even if we accept that a theory can be falsified in this way, we might still want to claim that some theories are interesting and merit careful consideration even after they have been falsified. They may still offer interesting insights or helpful ways of looking at the world. To a strict deductionist, once a theory is falsified it must be abandoned in favour of a modified version or a different theory altogether. Some thinkers claim that it might be worth hanging on to the old theory, even if this means keeping it alongside a new or different one.

A case in point is Newton's theory of gravity. Newton's laws were accepted in science for a long time because they were able to explain a lot about how the world, and indeed the universe, worked. There was evidence, however, that might have been seen as falsifying the laws. In particular the orbit of Mercury did not behave as they predicted. But to abandon the laws altogether for this reason would have left science with no account at all of the movement of bodies. So the useful but obviously flawed account was kept, together with the evidence that technically falsified it. This data was eventually explained by Einstein's general theory of relativity. Newton's theory is so accurate and explanatory, however, that it is still used today in calculations for space travel. Even though it has been falsified it is still useful.

Theorists in all fields generally accept that they are unlikely to come up with a definitive account of their subject matter that will be proved to be correct and will be universally accepted. Indeed it makes little sense to talk of proving any type of theory. If you take the inductive approach you can find as much data as you like to support your theory, but it will always remain probabilistic. As we have seen, if you are deductive in your method the issue of proof simply does not arise. A valid theory is one that has not been falsified – yet. What makes a theory of language or of anything else interesting is the light it can shed on a particular area of inquiry: the particular way of looking at the matter that it suggests. Karl Popper argued that 'Theories are nets cast to catch what we call "the world"; to rationalize, to explain, and to master it' (Popper, 2002, pp. 37–8).

Both deduction and induction have proved to be important tools for language study. When we look at some of the ideas of Noam Chomsky in more detail in Chapter 2 we will see how the deductive method has informed his studies and his conclusions. Chomsky once defended his method against the accusation that it was too speculative and not properly grounded in observation by arguing that serious hypotheses, about language or anything else, will always go beyond the available evidence; 'if they did not, they would be without interest' (Chomsky, 1969, p. 66). For Chomsky it is the big, risky claims made possible by deduction that are the most interesting, not the generalisations of induction. Induction too has its advocates in linguistics. It is used in those branches of linguistics that are based on the analysis of large amounts of language data. We briefly considered this approach in relation to corpus linguistics earlier in this chapter. Induction is also used – in fact is a guiding principle – in conversation analysis. This is based on careful attention to recorded examples of genuine conversations, and is concerned with the structures and patterns found in even the most casual of conversations. Here is a passage from an introduction to conversation analysis (CA) that is particularly concerned with the issue of methodology:

> CA views the empirical conduct of speakers as the central resource out of which analysis must develop. Furthermore, what is said provides not only the data underlying analysis, but also the evidence for hypotheses and conclusions: it is participants' conduct itself that must provide evidence for the presence of units, existence of patterns, and formation of rules. To this end, CA searches for recurrent patterns, distributions, and forms of organization in large corpora of talk (Schiffrin, 1994, p. 236).

For a conversation analyst, then, the raw data of recorded and transcribed conversation is not used simply as a test for theories of conversation. It is actually the driving force behind any legitimate analysis. If the analyst is interested in identifying patterns and rules, these must be built up from the evidence of the data. The analyst must proceed by making generalisations about the relevant data. For that reason 'large corpora' or huge amounts of data are necessary. It will not be possible just to try out a series of isolated examples to check whether a particular theory is falsified. On the contrary, the more data there is, the stronger will be the analyst's conviction in the conclusions drawn from it. This is clearly recognisable as the inductive scientific method.

Both induction and deduction are still used, and actively defended, as methods in language study. As with so many of the issues and debates we are considering here, it is not a case of one being necessarily right and the other wrong, or of deciding conclusively which is the better. Both methods have things to recommend them and can offer interesting insights into language. The important thing is to be aware of what type of method any individual linguist is using, and to remember the limitations of this method and its possible implications for the resultant account of language. The choices of method that thinkers make are generally related to what they consider to be the most important aspects of the subject under study. So linguists who believe it is most important to study how people generally use language in different situations will be drawn to the inductive method. Those interested in explaining language in terms of unseen but powerful mental capacities will be drawn to the deductive method. So the choice of method often depends on individual theorists' views of what language essentially is. We will consider this issue in the next chapter.

1.3   Further reading

See Clark (2006, ch. 1) for a discussion of issues that are relevant to the question 'What is a language?', which, as we have seen, should be distinguished from the question 'What is language?'; for a description of the processes and methodologies of sociolinguistics, which we have considered in relation to different types of data; and for practical advice on how to use these in your own research. In Chapter 2 of that volume there is a discussion of the methodology of conversation analysis, which we have considered in relation to the inductive method.

Language is . . . **2**

It is time now to look at some of the possible answers to the question 'What is language?' Linguists have come up with a huge variety of ideas in relation to this question. Here we will group some of the most important of these ideas under three headings: we will consider accounts of language that rely on the claim that language is a type of behaviour, that it is a state of mind, and that it is a means of communication. This might appear to be a rather odd set of distinctions to make because the three claims are not necessarily mutually exclusive. Many people, indeed many language theorists, would be happy to agree that using language means engaging in a particular type of behaviour, as well as going through particular mental processes and communicating with others. The differences between the three categories are largely differences of emphasis. Thinkers have made different decisions about which of these features is the essential or defining property of language, and which are secondary or incidental. They have also made different decisions about what we need to explain and what we can afford to ignore when we think about language.

Thinking about language does not of course stop at deciding how to define and explain language itself. There are all sorts of other questions that have concerned linguists and philosophers of language over the centuries. Possible answers to these questions are interesting in their own right, and for what they suggest about language. But because language is so central to what it is to be a human being, they can also go beyond this and tell us things about ourselves. They relate to topics of discussion that people often find fascinating, regardless of whether or not they are professional theorists. These topics include how we think, how we learn about the world around us, how we relate to each other and the extent to which we are different from or the same as other species of animal. We will consider a number of these topics in

Part II. As we will see, the ways in which thinkers have addressed these interesting, far-reaching topics have often been influenced by the positions they have taken on the nature of language. The decisions that thinkers take about language, including how to complete the sentence 'Language is . . .' can have consequences for what they say about many aspects of what it is to be a human being.

The views on language that we are about to explore come from a wide range of sources. They have been developed over the last few decades, and in some cases over the last few centuries, by thinkers from the various areas of study that take an interest in language. Wherever they come from, these views all have an impact on how current language theorists work. The present-day discipline of linguistics is conventionally divided into a number of branches: syntax, sociolinguistics, pragmatics and so on. Each field is based on particular assumptions about what language is, and these assumptions are generally drawn from the broad categories of definition we will be considering here. It is not always easy to relate each branch of linguistics to one distinct definition. Broadly speaking syntax, which is to do with the grammatical rules that exist in the minds of the speakers of a language, is based on the assumption that language is best defined as a state of mind. As we have already seen, sociolinguistics takes into account the situations in which language is used and the purposes to which it is put, so this branch draws on the idea that language is primarily a means of communication.

The assumptions underlying pragmatics are harder to explain with a single definition. Pragmatics is the study of how meaning is conveyed between speakers of a language in particular contexts, so it certainly draws on the idea that language is a means of communication. But many linguists working in the field of pragmatics subscribe to the idea that a language exists – independently of any individual instance of use – in the minds of its speakers. In fact some types of pragmatic theory depend on this idea, because they distinguish between aspects of a communicated message that are part of this independent language and aspects that depend simply on context. As a result many linguists working with this theoretical framework draw most strongly on the idea that language is a state of mind, despite their obvious interest in the processes of communication. We will look briefly at two pragmatic theories in Chapters 7 and 8.

Here we will consider some of the precise influences of our three definitions of present-day linguistics as we go along. And we will start by looking at the origins and implications of the idea that the study of language is at heart the study of a particular type of behaviour.

2.1   Language is a type of behaviour

While the ideas we are about to consider have had an important and ongoing impact on the study of language, some of the thinkers who pioneered them were not primarily linguists but were working in the fields of anthropology and psychology. These disciplines are both concerned with the study of human beings: either in the varieties of human ways of life or in the motivations of human action. So the study of language has been a natural extension of the interests of anthropologists and psychologists. To them it seems obvious that describing the activities of human beings includes describing language. In fact it would be difficult to think of a single type of activity that better summed up the human condition than the use of language.

Therefore the founding assumption of the work we will be looking at in this chapter is that language is a human activity, to be studied alongside and as far as possible in the same way as other human activities. The data for this type of study then is the observable forms of behaviour that people engage in when they use language. The aim is to give an adequate account and explanation of this behaviour, and thereby find out all about language. This is not just an implicit principle of the work, or an incidental side issue. Thinkers working in this tradition have made a point of arguing that it is necessary when studying language to start and end with observable behaviour.

This point of view necessarily has implications for the way in which the study of language is conducted. The following are the opening paragraphs from a book by the linguist Geoffrey Sampson. He begins by making it clear that language is behaviour, and then goes on to make some very definite claims about how it should be studied:

> Language is people talking and writing. It is a concrete, tangible aspect of human behaviour. So, if we want to deepen our understanding of language, our best way forward is to apply the same empirical techniques which have deepened our understanding of other observable aspects of the universe during the four centuries since Galileo.
>
> Look, listen. Summarize what you see and hear in hypotheses which are general enough to lead to predictions about future observations. Keep on testing your hypotheses. When new observations disconfirm some of them, look for alternative explanations compatible with all the evidence so far available; and then test these explanations in their turn against further observational data. This is the empirical scientific method (Sampson, 2001, p. 1).

Sampson claims a scientific pedigree for his chosen methodology that goes right back to Galileo, the astronomer who first identified the fact that the earth revolves around the sun, and who is often seen as the founder of modern science. The start of the second paragraph is recognisably a summary of the inductive scientific method we studied in the previous chapter. Sampson argues that this is the scientifically respectable approach to any area of investigation, although it is interesting that there does seem to be a slight merging of this with falsification and the deductive method in the suggestion that new observations may 'disconfirm' hypotheses and lead to their being abandoned. Most importantly, for Sampson the study of language, like the study of any other topic, must be empirical.

An empirical study is one based on observable evidence. An empiricist is someone whose understanding of a topic is built up entirely from experience. We have already seen that observable evidence can serve as data in relation to a theory in a number of different ways. For an empiricist, any conclusions drawn must be based entirely in what you can observe for yourself in the data. That is, you must work inductively, drawing general conclusions from specific, observable evidence. Empiricists reject the deductive method because it goes beyond what you can tell from the data or what you can know from experience. In the words of Leonard Bloomfield, one of the most important empiricists in language study:

> The only useful generalizations about language are inductive generalizations. Features which we think ought to be universal may be absent from the very next language that becomes accessible. Some features, such as, for instance, the distinction of verb-like and noun-like words as separate parts of speech, are common to many languages, but lacking in others. The fact that some features are, at any rate, widespread, is worthy of notice and calls for an explanation; when we have adequate data about many languages, we shall have to return to the problem of general grammar and to explain these similarities and divergences, but this study, when it comes, will be not speculative but inductive (Bloomfield, 1935, p. 20).

Here Bloomfield is counselling extreme caution in any attempt to define the properties of a general grammar, or a set of rules that apply to all human languages. If we do try to do this, he warns, our efforts must be based on adequate data. That is, we must accumulate as much information as we can about the languages of the world, and only describe patterns and similarities that we can see in this information. Bloomfield's reference to 'the very next language that becomes accessible' is interesting from the point of view of methodology. He was working in the early part of the twentieth century in the tradition of comparative linguistics, which was concerned with describing of the different languages of the world. In America this was focused in particular on recording and describing the languages of native American tribes. Bloomfield advocated an approach to linguistic study based on fieldwork; the linguist should observe the behaviour of native speakers of the language within their own society. Claims about language were legitimate only if they were based on the meticulous observation and analysis of as much data as possible from individual languages.

Bloomfield's empiricism extended not just to his method of study but also to his views on how best to describe language, or what language actually was. For him, collecting and describing language data was the most appropriate thing to do because language consisted entirely of what could be observed. That is, language was the set of behaviours observable in a group of speakers. So Bloomfield's approach to language was 'materialist', or what he also referred to as 'mechanistic'. Materialists' accounts of language concentrated on the observable, or the physical, as the ultimate location of linguistic properties. They explicitly rejected any reference to mental processes or psychological intentions underlying the production of language data. Such features were not amenable to inductive study because they could be observed or recorded. But they were in any case irrelevant because language was just observable behaviour.

In the following example, the features Bloomfield included and the things that he omitted tell us a lot about his ideas on language:

> Suppose that Jack and Jill are walking down a lane. Jill is hungry. She sees an apple in a tree. She makes a noise with her larynx, tongue, and lips. Jack vaults the fence, climbs the tree, takes the apple, brings it to Jill, and places it in her hand. Jill eats the apple (ibid., p. 22).

There are a number of striking features in this short story, if we bear in mind that it is a linguist's account of an example of language use. At the centre of the story, when Jill speaks we are not told what she says. We are merely told that she makes a 'noise', and we are given details of the physical apparatus she uses to do this. We might wonder whether in contrast we are given too much information about what comes next. Jack and Jill's subsequent actions are described in great detail; can all this really be relevant to the linguistic example in question?

Bloomfield, of course, included just that information that he saw as relevant to describing the behaviour that made up language. For him language was the speech that people produced: the audible sounds that occurred in different contexts. The linguist should simply record these sounds, and not make any judgments about what the speaker intended by them or what they meant. Reference to the vocal organs was relevant because speech was a physical or mechanical process. Everything else in the story was not simply background or extraneous information. It was all part of what the linguist would observe when recording behaviour, and as such it should be included in the description. In the above extract the first three sentences do not just set the scene, they also describe what immediately preceded the event of speech, so they must hold the key to why those particular sounds occurred at that particular time. The actions that followed the speech are highly relevant because they tell us about the consequences of the speech, or the effect it had in the world.

For Bloomfield, then, empirical linguists had not completed their job if they just described the sounds that came out of a speaker's mouth. They should also explain the physical features of the context immediately preceding and following these sounds, including the behaviour of the speaker and of those affected by the speech. The set of features preceding the speech explained why those particular sounds were produced. The features that followed it explained what was achieved, or brought about, as a result of the speech. Taken together these two sets of features were the only source of information about the significance or meaning of the speech event itself. For an empirical linguist it was not appropriate to say anything about the meaning of words or phrases except with reference to these sets of features.

This was not to say that in any particular context it ought to be possible to predict what someone would say and what would happen next. Bloomfield readily admitted that this was not possible, because the set of circumstances that prompted any speech event were just too complex. In the above case they might include aspects of Jill's experience, going right back to childhood, the nature of her relationship with Jack and her own personality. Similarly the effects of her utterance might well depend on Jack's attitude towards her. But Bloomfield's claim was that it was at least in principle possible to explain speech, and therefore language, in terms of what prompted it and what consequences followed from it. An omniscient linguist with access to all the relevant knowledge, going right back to Jill's childhood, would be able to do this.

Bloomfield's account of language was heavily influenced by ideas that were current in psychology at the time he was working. In the middle decades of the twentieth century psychology was dominated by a school of thought that became known as behaviourism. The effects of behaviourism reached beyond psychology to related disciplines such as linguistics. One particular book that had a significant impact on linguistics was *Verbal Behavior* by B. F. Skinner (1957). We will look at this in Chapter 9 when we consider how children learn language. For the time being, a quick look at the main ideas of behaviourism will help us to understand the implications of explaining language in behaviourist terms.

As we might expect, behaviourism was stringently materialist. An account of any aspect of human behaviour had to be explained entirely in terms of observable physical processes. Behaviourist psychologists had no time for explanations that referred to minds, thought processes or emotions. These could not be observed directly and therefore had no place in scientific theories. Behaviourists tended to refer not to people but to organisms. This was because they believed that it ought to be possible to explain the behaviour of all types of animal, including human beings, in the same way. They were opposed to any attempts to make a special case for humans, or to refer to unempirical concepts such as human nature or human psychology. Human behaviour was basically no different from the behaviour of any other organism, apart from sometimes being more complex, and it had to be explained with the use of the same apparatus.

Behaviourist explanations generally made reference to the connection between a 'stimulus' and a 'response'. Some feature or set of features in a context served as the starting point or the trigger for a particular behaviour. This was the stimulus that was relevant to the behaviour under investigation, and the organism's observable behaviour that resulted from the stimulus was known as the response. Certain responses would be reinforced for the organism by having favourable consequences. These responses were likely to be repeated in the future when similar stimuli presented themselves. Other responses would not be reinforced, either having no significant consequences for the organism or having consequences that were unfavourable. Responses that were not reinforced were less likely to be repeated on subsequent occasions. Stimulus, response and reinforcement must all be physical phenomena, which were in principle at least available for inspection and description by the scientist.

For example, suppose we are describing a man eating crisps. The relevant stimulus here will be the physical sensation of hunger, which could if necessary be described mechanistically in terms of the secretion of gastric juices and so on. The man may also be stimulated by the sight of the packet of crisps. The man responds to these stimuli by the physical act of opening the packet and eating the crisps. There is an immediate consequence of these actions: he no longer feels hungry. This favourable consequence reinforces the act of eating crisps, so that in the future if the man is hungry and sees crisps again he will be disposed to eat them again. In fact the act of eating crisps has probably been prompted by the reinforcement of similar acts in the past. The scientist cannot observe or describe the man's hunger, but he can see the physical responses it produces. So for the behaviourist, hunger is a tendency, or a disposition, to eat food if it is available.

The same type of explanation must be applied to sensations other than hunger, and in some cases the behaviourist account can look very different from our normal understanding of human beings. Emotions such as anger could not figure in behaviourist accounts because they could not be directly observed, or explained in materialist terms. They certainly could not play any part in an explanation of behaviour. So for the behaviourist what we call anger was simply the disposition to behave aggressively, shout, and become red in the face. Similarly what we call sadness was the disposition to assume a particular facial expression, or to cry, or to withdraw from human company. What we call love was the disposition to make efforts to be in the presence of a particular individual, to act in ways that promoted that individual's well-being, and so on.

We can see a number of similarities to Bloomfield's account of language in this summary of behaviourism. There was his refusal to explain language in terms of anything hidden or mental. He concentrated instead on observable behaviour; for Bloomfield, language simply was speech. He also explained meaning in terms of observable causes and consequences. For instance, for Jill the relevant stimuli were her sensation of hunger and the sight of the apple in the tree across the fence. She responded to these with an act of speaking. This act had observable consequences: Jack went and got the apple for her. This success reinforced her action; she would be disposed to perform a similar act of speaking in similar circumstances in the future.

Using the ideas and principles of behaviourism to explain language is dependent on the assumption that language is first and last a form of behaviour. Linguists who make this assumption are committed to the view that language is not essentially different from any other form of behaviour. It exists in instances of what people do and how their behaviour affects others. This emphasis on consequence and effect formed a major part of Bloomfield's explanation of why we have language. Mary might have responded to seeing the apple by climbing the fence and picking it herself. But if this were physically difficult for her to do it would be beneficial for her to be able to use an act of speaking to influence a stronger person to do it for her. Language functions in society in this way. Groups of people do not all need to do everything individually for themselves. Rather, through language they are able to organise things so that individuals do what they are good at, both for themselves and for others.

The mid-twentieth-century work of the American philosopher W. V. O. Quine is highly relevant to this interest in the operation of language within a society. We looked briefly at Quine's ideas in Chapter 1, when we analysed his definition of language as a social art. We saw then that for Quine language consisted in what could be observed about how people interacted with each other in different social situations. Looking back at his words now, we can perhaps also recognise his restriction of meaning to 'men's dispositions to respond overtly to socially observable stimulations' as the outline of a fundamentally behaviourist account of language. The only way in which it is possible to talk about the meaning of any word or phrase is to describe the types of stimuli that typically prompt speakers to produce it in context.

But in Quine's work we are not looking at just another behaviourist account of language. Quine considered the implications of this approach, and drew some conclusions that are particularly interesting in connection with the question 'What is language?' To start with there was his rejection of any notion of meaning independent of behaviour, something that we touched on when we first looked at his definition of language. This attitude followed from a behaviourist approach to language, but Quine made it a more prominent part of his work than Bloomfield had done. This aspect of Quine's thinking about language is sometimes described as 'semantic scepticism'.

In any area of study the term scepticism is used to refer to an attitude of doubt or questioning; a sceptic is someone who is not committed to a belief, usually a belief in the existence of something. By adopting an attitude of semantic scepticism Quine was calling into doubt the existence of meaning itself. It is perfectly possible to describe the verbal responses that speakers typically produce, and perhaps how these are typically reinforced. To borrow Bloomfield's example, if linguists are interested in describing the phrase *Can I have an apple?* they might observe during the course of fieldwork that it is typically produced by speakers who are in the presence of a particular type of fruit. They might also observe that this piece of verbal behaviour is typically followed by an act of someone else handing the piece of fruit to the speaker, and that this act appears to reinforce the verbal behaviour. The description of the phrase *Can I have an apple?* will include reference to speakers' tendencies or dispositions to produce it in response to particular stimuli, and to the tendency of other speakers of the language to reinforce its production in particular ways. The description of the phrase will not, however, include any reference to the meaning of the phrase, which is independent of these tendencies. For Quine this independent notion of meaning had an intangible, almost a mystic quality about it that meant it has no place in serious – that is, scientific – discussions of language. It was not possible to observe or to have any direct evidence of this type of meaning, so it made no sense to make it part of an account of language.

Quine's semantic scepticism, his resistance to the idea that meaning existed in some way independently of individual instances of verbal behaviour, was an important component of his view of language in its own right. But it also had an implication that has proved even more significant, because of what it suggests about how we should assess and compare descriptions of a language. Quine labelled this implication the 'principle of indeterminacy of translation'. As the title suggests, it makes claims about translating between two different languages. But it is not just an idea about translation, interesting though that would be. Quine's principle is about the very nature of language itself.

As we have seen, for Quine parts of a language are meaningful to the extent that they tend to occur in response to certain stimuli and to be followed by certain types of reinforcement. A language is the collection of verbal behaviours of the speakers of that language. It follows that when learning a language, whether a first language or a second or subsequent language, a speaker's task is to learn to behave verbally in the same way as the other speakers of the language. The speaker's success in learning the language can be judged in terms of the extent to which he or she has developed the dispositions to respond to stimuli and to reinforce the responses of others in the same way as other speakers of the language.

Now consider the case of the linguist who wants to compare two different languages in order to be able to translate words and sentences from one into the other. Quine's semantic scepticism means that it will not do to look at the meaning of components of one language and compare them with the meaning of components of the other. There are no independent 'meanings' to be compared. As always in empirical linguistics, this task should be performed by means of field work involving the two languages. The linguist could record the patterns of stimulus, response and reinforcement apparent in one language and look for similar patterns in the other. If one particular piece of verbal behaviour in language *A* displays a similar pattern of stimulus, response and reinforcement to a piece of verbal behaviour in language *B*, it might be reasonable to propose the expression in language *A* as a translation of the expression in language *B*.

Note that this definition does not deal in certainties; it deals in what is similar and what is reasonable. It follows from Quine's semantic scepticism that the linguist will never be able to make a definite statement about how to translate an expression from one language into another; it simply makes no sense to worry about whether the expressions in the two languages have the same meaning because neither of them actually has any meaning at all. But although there can never be certainty in translation, some proposals for translations are more reliable than others. In particular, proposals about expressions that are clearly related to immediately observable stimuli in the environment are more reliable than those about expressions that are not so clearly linked to observable stimuli. The linguist can be more confident about proposing a translation for *There's a rabbit!*, for instance, than for *I'm contemplating the immortality of the soul*.

This lack of absolute certainty in translation is perhaps not too troubling. It is generally accepted that exact translation is an impossibility, and we will consider the reasons for this in Chapter 3. But Quine went further, suggesting that his principle of indeterminacy of translation implied that 'manuals for translating one language into another can be set up in divergent ways, all compatible with the totality of speech dispositions, yet incompatible with one another' (Quine, 1960, p. 27). Because there was no such thing as a single correct translation of any expression into another language, it was perfectly possible for two linguists engaged in fieldwork to come up with different, incompatible, systems for translating one language into another. They might both engage in extensive observations of the verbal behaviour of the two sets of speakers and make comparisons of the languages that were both fully workable in practice but were different from each other. What is most striking is that Quine saw this as a consequence of his principle that was not just possible but also totally reasonable. It would make no sense for the two linguists to argue about who had got the translation right, he claimed, because there was no such thing as a right translation, only one that explained the observable facts. If both translations explained the observable facts adequately, they were equally as good as each other.

Now we can think about what implications the principle of indeterminacy of translation has for the nature of language itself. The principle implies that it can never be legitimate to talk about two expressions having the same meaning, whether these are two expressions in different languages or two expressions in the same language. Quine's examples here are *bachelor* and *unmarried man*. In informal everyday language we might well say that these two expressions mean the same thing or have the same meaning. According to Quine, of course, this is not an empirically justified way of speaking because it implies that there is something, a meaning, that the two expressions have in common with each other. All that we can say is that the speakers of English generally display a disposition to respond with these two types of verbal behaviour to similar observable stimuli. That is, we tend to use these two expressions in similar ways.

More generally, since a language consists of dispositions to respond to stimuli, an account of any individual language will be accurate to the extent that it correctly describes this set of dispositions. Just as in the case of two different languages, it is entirely possible that two linguists will come up with two different translations, so in the case of a single language it is possible that there will be two different descriptions of the verbal behaviour of its speakers. It is possible that these descriptions will differ from each other, and in fact be incompatible with each other, but will both account for the facts of observable behaviour. In such cases, Quine claimed, there is no place for arguing that one description of a language is correct, or is better than the other description. An accurate account of the dispositions to verbal behaviour is all that can be hoped for from a description of a language. To claim otherwise would be to argue that there is a truth about language beyond individual instances of behaviour, or that meaning exists in exactly the way that Quine disallowed.

Quine's insistence that two accounts of a language that described the behaviour of its speakers equally well were just as good as each other is one of the ways in which his views were as different as they could be from those of some other prominent thinkers about language. Their alternative ways of thinking, which will be our main focus in the next section, were put forward so forcefully, and have been so influential since the middle part of the twentieth century, that nowadays thinkers working on language tend to be reluctant to describe themselves as behaviourists. They tend not to want to be associated with the more extreme aspects of behaviourism: the claim that there was nothing to be said about human beings other than to describe their observable behaviour, and the accompanying rejection of any notion of unobservable mental processes. Nevertheless there is still work on language being produced in which we can identify some of the ideas we have considered in this section. In particular there is work that does not accept the more extreme antimentalism of behaviourism but goes along with the insistence on sticking to observable behaviour, and on ruling out any notion of language or meaning as existing independently of that behaviour. This is why our consideration of behaviourism is crucial to understanding present-day thinking about language, and is not of marginal or merely historical interest.

One current approach to language that rules out any notion of meaning independent of use is the school of thought known as integrational linguistics. Integrational linguists would not necessarily describe themselves as behaviourists, and indeed some of them have been overtly critical of work by previous thinkers such as Bloomfield and Quine. The term integrational is often defined in opposition to segregational, which is a label these linguists use to describe much of the history of thought about language. Segregational linguists rely on the assumption that language has some form of independent existence: that it can be isolated or segregated from any individual context or situation and studied in its own right. Integrational linguist Roy Harris summarises the difference as follows:

> The alternative approach, the integrational approach, sees language as manifested in a complex of human abilities and activities that are all integrated in social interaction, often intricately so and in such a manner that it makes little sense to segregate the linguistic from the non-linguistic components (Harris, 1998, p. 6).

So integrationists insist on seeing people's behaviour as a whole. It is a futile activity to try to separate out aspects of a piece of human interaction and say 'This is linguistic' and 'This is non-linguistic'. Language is no more and no less than the set of behaviours and abilities to behave that can be observed in any human society. Integrationalism rules out the reductive move of isolating some aspect of that set as the proper focus of study in linguistics. The study of language – that is, the study of communication – must include the study of contexts in which it takes place, the triggers that cause it to occur and the effects it has within the society.

In a slightly earlier account of the distinction between integrationism and segregationism, Harris concentrates on the notion of the linguistic 'sign'. This is an important element of much traditional thinking about language, and one that we will consider in more detail in Chapter 5. A sign is a linguistic element, such as a word, that exists as part of a particular language and can be employed by speakers of that language to communicate meaning in context. For Harris this is exactly where segregational linguistics gets it wrong:

> For the segregationist, communication presupposes signs: signs and sign systems exist apart from and prior to the communicational purposes to which they may or may not be put. For the integrationist, on the contrary, signs presuppose communication: they are its products, not its prerequisites (Harris, 1996, p. 7).

For the integrationist, then, language exists only in a series of individual, unique acts of communication. Linguistic signs, as far as they exist at all, are produced only by these individual acts; they are created each time people communicate. It is simply wrong to think of signs as in some way existing prior to or independent of the context in which they occur. It follows that it is equally wrong to think about the same word or the same sentence being used on different occasions; words and sentences are properties of particular acts of communication, so a sentence that forms part of one act of communication cannot be the same as a sentence that belongs to a different act of communication. In support of this argument, Harris points out that what might traditionally be described as the same sentence can have widely different communicative effects, depending on the context. He offers the example of a sign displayed in a coach station: 'All Tours Start Here'. The meaning of this notice, he argues, in entirely dependent on its context; it is not just a case of the word *here* being tied to the physical location of the sign:

> To make sense of this *all* has to be treated as no less 'context-dependent' than *here* (or *tours*, or *start*). (If travelers thought otherwise, the ensuing traffic problems would rapidly bring all services to a halt and cause chaos on the roads for miles around.) (Ibid., pp. 157–8.)

In Chapter 7 we will consider the importance of context in determining meaning, and the different ways in which linguists have responded to this.

Certainly integrationism is not the only possible way of accounting for it. There are a number of accounts of meaning that allow for the importance of context while still belonging to what Harris would describe as segregationist linguistics.

For the integrational linguist, then, signs exist only as and when they are created in context in individual acts of communication; they are defined by the circumstances of their production and reception. One other corollary of this is that it makes no sense to attempt to distinguish between signs that are 'linguistic' and signs that are 'non-linguistic'. For an integrationist, everything that appears to function as a sign in a piece of communication must be treated as having the same status. A word or sentence is no different from a thumbs-up, a handshake or even a ring on a doorbell. All exist, and are significant, simply as they occur in communication. Like behaviourism, then, integrational linguistics does not see anything special about language. It is no different from any other form of communicative behaviour, and any account of language ought to be of the same type and work in the same way as accounts of other types of communicative behaviour. The ideas that will be our focus in the next section, based on the view that language is a state of mind, lead to an entirely different attitude towards the status of language. In this approach, language is seen as a unique and distinctive area of study. The specific features and regularities of language are like nothing else that we come across in the study of human beings.

2.2   Language is a state of mind

In this section we will be looking at some ideas about language that are very different from the ones we have just been considering. They are most closely associated with the American linguist Noam Chomsky, whose work we looked at briefly in Chapter 1. Chomsky has certainly not been the only person to hold the views discussed here, nor has he been the only linguist to contribute to their development. But he was responsible for introducing these ideas into linguistics in the middle part of the twentieth century, and his name almost invariably comes up in any discussion of the claim that language is a state of mind. So in this chapter we will follow the convention of using the term Chomskyan linguistics as a convenient shorthand for this particular approach to the study of language.

We will start with a passage from one of Chomsky's many books on the subject. This is a longish extract, but it is worth reading because it highlights some of the principal differences between Chomskyan linguistics and the approaches we considered in the last section, and it also gives an overview of some of the ideas we will need to think about in this one.

Human language, in its normal use, is free from the control of independently identifiable external stimuli or internal states and is not restricted to any practical communicative function, in contrast, for example, to the pseudo language of animals. It is thus free to serve as an instrument of free thought and self-expression. The limitless possibilities of thought and imagination are reflected in the creative aspect of language use. The language provides finite means but infinite possibilities of expression constrained only by rules of concept formation and sentence formation, these being in part particular and idiosyncratic but in part universal, a common human endowment (Chomsky, 1966, p. 29).

In this passage Chomsky is actually describing a set ideas about language developed in the seventeenth century. However he makes it quite clear that he believes modern linguists would do well to learn from these ideas, and in effect he is drawing attention to them in order to claim a sound philosophical ancestry for his own approach to linguistics. This passage works just as well as a summary of some of Chomsky's own preoccupations.

The first thing to notice is the way in which Chomsky distances himself from behaviourism. When he tells us that language is 'free from the control of independently identifiable external stimuli or internal states' he is ruling out the claim that was fundamental to behaviourist accounts of language: that every time someone uses language there is an identifiable trigger or cause. As we have seen, for behaviourists it was at least in principle possible to predict any piece of behaviour, including linguistic behaviour, given enough information about the relevant stimuli. These stimuli could include changes in the immediate environment of the organism and also of the physical state of the organism itself. In Bloomfield's (1935) example of Jill asking Jack to fetch her an apple, her behaviour was prompted by the appearance of an apple tree in her field of vision and by her own physical sensation of hunger. For Chomskyan linguists it would make no sense to ask what acted as the stimulus for what someone has said. The use of language is free and spontaneous and therefore can never be predicted.

This insistence on spontaneity is part of a much larger theme in Chomskyan linguistics: the special nature of language. For behaviourists language may have been unusually complex but it was basically a form of behaviour like any other, and amenable to the types of description and explanation applied to any form of behaviour. For Chomsky, when people use language they are doing something unique and very specific. Most importantly, this is because what people must know in order to be able to use a language is a unique and very specific type of knowledge. This last point goes right to the heart of Chomskyan linguistics, and we will consider it in more detail later in this section.

Closely related to Chomsky's rejection of behaviourism is his claim that language is 'not restricted to any practical communicative function' (Chomsky, 1966, p. 29). Behaviourist descriptions of language included reference not just to the stimuli that prompted linguistic behaviour, but also to the consequences that the behaviour had, or in technical terms the 'reinforcement' that the speaker experienced as a result. Part of Bloomfield's (1935) explanation of Jill's linguistic behaviour in relation to the apple was the observation that her remark was followed by Jack's action of climbing the tree and bringing the apple to her. For Chomsky it is not necessary to identify any such practical consequences when explaining language. This is not to deny that people often do use language to communicate their wants to other people in order to get them to behave in particular ways. But language is not always used for such practical reasons, and so there is no need to make this a requirement of the definition of language. Sometimes people use language without any identifiable practical purpose: to entertain or simply to pass the time. Indeed language need not be used in order to communicate at all. Far from existing only in individual acts of communication, it exists independently of any such act and would continue to exist if it were never used to communicate. This startling claim, not surprisingly, has proved to be one of the most controversial aspects of Chomsky's thinking about language. At first sight it seems extraordinary, even eccentric, to claim that communication is not a necessary feature of language. But as we will see it is in fact a necessary consequence of Chomsky's view that language should be defined primarily in relation not to what people do but to what is in their minds.

It is striking that Chomsky contrasts his picture of human language with 'the pseudo language of animals' (ibid.). This phrase indicates that he does not believe that the various communication systems used by animals merit being described as languages. Rather animal communication is prompted by identifiable triggers and aimed at practical consequences. It lacks the spontaneity of human language and, most importantly, it exists in the ways in which animals behave, not in what is in their minds. In Chapter 10 we will think further about different animal communication systems and whether or not they qualify as languages. At this stage we should note that Chomsky's ideas about language rely on something that was explicitly ruled out from behaviourist accounts: belief in the unique and specific properties of human nature. Knowing a language and having the freedom to use it spontaneously are simply part of what it is to be human.

So far Chomsky's definition of language might seem to be rather negative. We have heard quite a lot about how not to define language: as a response to particular stimuli, as a form of behaviour or as a means of communication. But we have not yet heard much about what language actually is; we do not yet have much of an answer to our question 'What is language?' Chomsky begins to provide his answer in the next sentence of the paragraph we are considering, when he explains that the fact that language is not restricted to practical communication means that it is 'free to serve as an instrument of free thought and self-expression' (ibid.). For Chomsky language exists first and foremost in the mind and is used above all in thought and expressing our ideas to ourselves. While the same system is also used to express ideas to other people and communicate with them, this is not its primary or its most frequent function. In later writings Chomsky expresses this idea particularly strongly, going so far as to claim that language is a mental state that only coincidentally has a secondary, derived function in communication (Chomsky, 1986). Certainly, for Chomsky language is primarily a state of mind; it exists as a set of specific knowledge in the minds of individual speakers. This perhaps sheds a bit more light on Chomsky's claim that communication does not need to take place for language to exist. According to this view, all that is needed for a language to exist is for there to be one person in existence who knows that language. For Chomsky, when Robinson Crusoe was alone on his island there was language because Crusoe was a speaker of English (ibid.). For a linguist who believes that language consists of behaviour, or at least of communicative speech, there could be no language on the island because Crusoe had no one to communicate with.

The creative aspect of language use follows from the fact that language is primarily a vehicle for thought. It is also one of the most important features of language for Chomsky, and one to which he refers frequently when discussing what he sees as the errors of alternative accounts. The possibilities of human thought seem to be limitless; we can think or imagine whatever we choose. And whatever we can think we can put into words. Language enables us to express a potentially infinite variety of thoughts and, if we choose to communicate those ideas, it allows others to understand those thoughts. In our daily lives we may hear things said that we have heard many times before, but we will probably also come across what are known as 'novel sentences'. It is a fairly good bet that you have never before heard or read the sentence *The queen of the North Pole is in a terrible state over the revolt among the penguins.* But now that you have read it you are perfectly able to understand what thought it is expressing, however unlikely you may find it.

This is one of Chomsky's main arguments against any theory of language that explains it in terms of a series of learned responses that have been successively reinforced. Your understanding of the sentence about the queen of the North Pole cannot be based on previous experience, because you are very unlikely to have come across it before. Similarly your ability to produce an infinite number of novel sentences suggests that your linguistic behaviour is not based simply on a repertoire of appropriate responses that you have built up through experience. Rather there must be a certain type of knowledge that speakers of a language share and are able to apply to the production and interpretation of an infinite number of possible sentences. In other words language must provide the 'finite means but infinite possibilities of expression' that Chomsky mentions next (Chomsky, 1966, p. 29). The means – that is, the knowledge that speakers are in possession of when they are fully able to speak and understand a language – must be finite because the human mind is capable only of finite knowledge. But that finite knowledge must be capable of producing an infinite variety of expressions in the language, because the human mind is capable of producing an infinite variety of new thoughts. We have seen that for Chomsky a language is a set of knowledge, and we are now getting closer to a definition of what that set of knowledge is. The speakers of a language do not know all the sentences of a language. In fact this would be impossible because the sentences of a language are infinite in number but the human mind is finite. What these speakers do know is the means, or the appropriate equipment, that gives them the capability to produce and understand the infinity of sentences.

The linguistic equipment in the minds of the speakers of a language consists in 'rules of concept formation and sentence formation' (ibid.). Knowing a language means knowing a set of rules that determine how the sentences of the language are put together, along with knowledge of the individual words the language contains. Knowing the set of rules allows us to distinguish between strings of words that are sentences of the language and strings of words that are not. When you read the sentence about the queen of the North Pole, you knew more than just what it meant. Although you may not have stopped to think about it, you also knew that, however unlikely it sounded in terms of real world events, it was certainly a grammatical sentence of the language. It is also likely that you have never before come across the string of words *Queen the North Pole the of terrible state a in revolt the over penguins the among is*. This contains exactly the same words as the previous example, but as a speaker of English you know that this particular string of words is not a grammatical sentence of English. This is because, although you may not be consciously aware of it when you make that judgment of ungrammaticality, you know a series of rules about how sentences are put together in English. You know, for instance, that determiners such as *the* and *a* always come before nouns in noun phrases. You know that prepositions such as *of, in* and *over* always come before noun phrases in prepositional phrases. You know that English is an SVO (subject followed by verb followed by object) language. All these rules are broken in the jumbled example, explaining why it does not qualify as a sentence of English.

We saw in Section 1.1 that in Chomskyan linguistics the intuitions of a native speaker are acceptable, indeed the best possible type of data when studying language. Chomsky's version of what language is explains this. By using intuitions, whether their own or someone else's, linguists are accessing information about the knowledge in the mind of a speaker of the language, which is precisely to access information about the language itself.

So far we have been considering the rules that make up a single language, namely English. Of course we can extend the claims made so far to other languages; any language consists of a finite set of rules that specify what are the grammatical sentences of that language and that exist in the mind of any speaker of that language. But Chomsky's claims are rather more ambitious than this. We get a hint of this in the paragraph we are considering here, when he tells us that the rules of a language are 'in part particular and idiosyncratic but in part universal' (ibid.). Here 'particular and idiosyncratic' refers to rules that belong to just one language. 'Universal' refers to rules that belong to all human languages; that is, some linguistic rules are common to all the languages of the world. In his work on language Chomsky has increasingly claimed that most of the important rules of language are universal, and that the differences between languages are minor, even trivial. There are of course differences between the vocabularies of languages, and certain local differences in how phrases and sentences are put together, but the major important structural properties of language are constant across societies, continents, and time.

A central feature of Chomskyan linguistics is the existence of universal grammar (UG), which specifies what counts as a grammatical sentence not just in a particular language but in any human language. For instance it is claimed that all languages have words that belong to particular categories, such as noun, verb and adjective. They all have specific ways in which these words are combined into phrases and then into sentences. The ways in which individual languages combine words and phrases do of course vary, but according to the theory of UG they vary within particular parameters. All human languages operate according to a restricted range of possibilities within these parameters. UG in effect specifies what is and what is not possible in human language. If this claim is true, then no human language should include a sentence that is not consistent with the rules of UG, and native speakers of all languages should be consistent in making grammaticality judgments in keeping with UG. This is a hugely ambitious hypothesis. Since the mid-twentieth century a lot of research in Chomskyan linguistics has gone into attempting to determine the rules of UG, and establishing their applicability across languages.

The final claim that Chomsky makes in the paragraph we are considering is just as powerful as the claim about the existence of UG, and is closely related to it. Anyone who claims the existence of UG must be able to explain how it is that all human languages have certain properties in common. It can hardly be a matter of coincidence. Rather there must be something about human beings that means only some of the many types of system that are possible will actually occur as human language. This is precisely what Chomsky claims: that UG has the power that it does over all human languages because it is a necessary component of the human mind; it is 'a common human endowment' (ibid.). In the terms we were using earlier, UG is part of human nature. It is literally in our genes; we are born with linguistic knowledge that is unconscious and unrealised, but will eventually determine many of the features of our language. Something that is inborn, or part of our genetic endowment, is often described as being innate, and this particular aspect of Chomsky's ideas about language has come to be referred to as the innateness hypothesis (IH). Chomsky himself has tended to avoid this phrase because of the erroneous implication that all other accounts of language deny that anything is innate, but nevertheless it has stuck, and we will use it here.

Looking into the implications of this one paragraph from Chomsky's writings has taken us quite a long way towards understanding some of the main features that make his thinking about language distinctive. We have seen that he describes language primarily as a state of mind, or more specifically as a special type of knowledge that is unique to human beings and is remarkably similar across the world because it results from a genetic predisposition. We have also seen that he rejects a number of other possible answers to the question 'What is language?' Language is not defined by the circumstances in which it is used or the communicative purposes to which it is put. It is manifest not primarily in speech or writing but in thought.

There are of course many other things to be said about Chomsky's thinking, and many aspects of it that we will not be able to cover in this section. But we will look at two specific questions that are raised by the above summary, questions that are particularly relevant to understanding Chomsky's views on what language actually is. Firstly, if language exists in the mind separately from speech and writing, we need to think a bit more about what the relationship is between the state of mind and the act of speaking. That is, we should consider how Chomsky answers the question that his theory of language raises: what is the relationship between language and the use of language? Secondly, we need to think in a little more detail about what it is that we know when we know a language. If language really does exist primarily as a set of knowledge in the mind of a speaker, any account of language must tell us what that set of knowledge is. We have seen that it can be defined as a finite set of rules that specify an infinite set of sentences, but there is still a lot more to be said about what those rules are and how they operate. So the second major question that Chomsky's theory of language raises can be summarised as follows: what does knowledge of language consist of? The remainder of this section will be concerned with looking at Chomsky's answers to these two questions.

Work in Chomskyan linguistics often includes discussion of the difference between 'language' and 'the use of language'. This highlights yet again just how significant linguists' decisions about the best answer to the question 'What is language?' are to how they go about discussing language. If language is a state of mind then the things that we can observe people doing, their speaking and writing, are examples of how people use language, not of language itself. Therefore the nature of the relationship between language and the use of language is a perfectly legitimate in fact a very important topic for discussion. For many other linguists the topic is not so much unimportant as meaningless. Those who view language as a type of behaviour do not allow any distinction between language and use of language. When we observe someone speaking or writing we are simply observing language itself. Language consist of the many things that a group of people within a society do. It makes no sense to ask questions about a language that is separate from what people do, or to worry about how the observable phenomena in that society relate to language as an unobservable mental phenomenon.

There is a specialist vocabulary in Chomskyan linguistics that avoids the cumbersome phrases 'language' and 'the use of language'. In Chomsky's writings the terms competence and performance are generally used in discussions of the distinction we are considering. The use of these terms is problematic because Chomsky himself has more or less abandoned them. In later writings he adopted instead the terms I-language (or internalised language) and E-language (or externalised language). However in discussions of Chomskyan linguistics the terms competence and performance are still often used and we will follow this practice here. In fact a lot of what Chomsky claimed about this distinction in his early writings is still relevant to his later distinction between I-language and E-language.

Competence is a speaker's knowledge of his or her language. It is what we know when we can be said to know a language: the set of rules that enable us to produce and interpret sentences, and to judge which strings of words are and which are not grammatical sentences of our language. Performance is what we do on those occasions when we use our linguistic competence in communicating with others. It is the collection of observable acts of speech and writing. Remember that for Chomsky communication is not an essential and is perhaps only a coincidental feature of language. He makes it clear in many of his writings that the proper focus of study in linguistics is competence. Linguists should be primarily concerned with describing and explaining what is in the mind of a speaker of a language, because this is language. Performance is not language. Linguists may sometimes look at the things that people say and write because of the clues that these things give them about language. But those linguists should be cautious about relying too heavily on information from performance, because linguistic competence is only one of the things that affect it. What people say on particular occasions depends in part on their knowledge of the language, but it also depends on a whole range of other factors. These might include, in different contexts, the nature of the relationship between speaker and hearer, the level of background noise, the speaker's past experiences, and even facts such as how tired the speaker is or how much he or she has had to drink. None of these factors are part of the language itself; none of them should properly be described as linguistic. Therefore linguists should always be aware that when they are looking at performance data they do not have direct or unadulterated access to information about the language.

The many non-linguistic factors that contribute to performance mean that speakers do not always produce utterances that they would themselves accept as grammatical sentences of their language. Because of lapses of memory, or nervousness, or being distracted while we are speaking, we often say things that do not accurately reflect our linguistic competence; given a chance we would correct these mistakes as we correct what we have written before we print or send it. In these cases, Chomsky argues, we should attend to speakers' judgments of what is and what is not grammatical, rather than to what they produce in speech. Speakers' judgments give us a more accurate picture of the language because actual instances of language use may be affected by so-called performance errors that are nothing to do with the language itself. Similarly, just because something does not occur in performance does not mean that it is not a grammatical sentence of the language. We have seen that, because of their linguistic competence, speakers are good judges of grammaticality. But they are also good judges of acceptability, because of aspects of their knowledge and experience of the world that have nothing to do with language. There are many sentences that conform to the rules of the grammar but speakers would judge as unacceptable, perhaps because they were obscene or did not describe a possible situation in the real world. Chomsky's own famous example of a grammatical but unacceptable sentence is 'Colorless green ideas sleep furiously' (Chomsky, 1957, p. 15). It is perfectly in keeping with the grammatical rules of English, as any speaker of the language will confirm, but it makes no sense. That is, it is nearly impossible to imagine a context in which it might actually be used.

In a famous passage in an early work Chomsky argues that ideally the linguist's ultimate goal should be to be able to abstract away from all the interference from non-linguistic factors that accompanies performance, and study just competence. The linguist's subject should be the 'ideal speaker-listener, in a completely homogeneous speech-community . . . unaffected by such grammatically irrelevant conditions as memory limitations, distractions, shifts of attention and interest, errors' (Chomsky, 1965, p. 3). That is, the linguist must try to ignore performance errors and concentrate only on the effects of competence.

The ideal situation that Chomsky is describing is ideal in the scientific sense. He is expressing the belief that linguists can study language only if they ignore all factors that interfere with the understanding of language in practice. It would be ideal if linguists could study language without interference from performance errors, just as it would be ideal if scientists could study gravity without interference from air resistance. This is not to claim that it would be ideal if we lived in a world where there were no performance factors, any more than it is to claim that it would be ideal if we lived in a world without air. The modifier 'grammatically' is significant here. Chomsky is not insisting that performance factors are irrelevant in society, in communication or to an understanding of human beings. Rather he is saying that they are irrelevant to the study of grammar as a mental structure, which for him is the appropriate topic of linguistics. Nevertheless this particular passage has proved one of the most controversial in all of Chomsky's writings about language. We will look at some responses and objections to it in the next section.

In the previous section we looked at a criticism by Roy Harris (1998) of linguistics as a discipline: that it does not tell us everything we need to know about communication. A Chomskyan defence of linguistics would not deny this. It would argue that the study of language – that is, of competence – does not by any means tell us everything about communication, and nor should it. There are many aspects of communication that are not determined by linguistic competence. But the narrow scope of linguistics is not a weakness to the Chomkyan linguist. Linguistics is not primarily concerned with explaining a subpart of communication, which might indeed be a rather restrictive goal. Rather it is concerned with explaining the whole of a rich, complex and specific aspect of the structure of the human mind. We saw in the previous section that empirical accounts of language such as those by Bloomfield (1935) and Quine (1960), which restrict themselves to the observable phenomena of language, are labelled 'materialist'. In opposition to this, Chomskyan linguistics is sometimes referred to as 'mentalist' linguistics.

In Section 1.1 we considered some of the implications of mentalist linguistics in relation to data. We have also seen that for Chomsky the mental state or the set of knowledge that constitutes a language consists of a finite set of rules that are capable of producing an infinite set of sentences. In finding out about these rules the linguist is finding out about the grammar of the particular language under investigation. That is, a grammar is what people know when they know a language; grammar is primarily a mental phenomenon. Chomsky makes it clear that the grammar of a language can be investigated only by means of careful analysis of the sentences that it produces. That is why speakers' intuition is such an important source of data in Chomskyan linguistics. By finding out about which strings of words speakers judge to be grammatical or ungrammatical, linguists are finding out about what the rules of their mental grammar allow and do not allow. No more direct evidence about the grammar is available. Linguists cannot ask speakers about their knowledge of the language, or contemplate their own mental states introspectively, because the rules of the grammar are not available to consciousness. Chomsky expresses this idea in the following sentence: 'Notice, incidentally, that a person is not generally aware of the rules that govern sentence-interpretation in the language that he knows; nor, in fact, is there any reason to suppose that the rules can be brought to consciousness' (Chomsky, 1971, p. 73). The grammatical rules proposed in Chomskyan linguistics are therefore not intended to be recognisable to speakers. They are attempts to describe the inaccessible knowledge that must be in operation in order to produce the accessible judgments about grammaticality and interpretation.

The type of grammar described and investigated in Chomskyan linguistics is often referred to as generative grammar. This name reflects the fact that a goal of Chomskyan linguistics is to establish a set of rules that are capable of producing, or of generating, all and only the sentences of the language. So, for instance, there is a generative rule in English: $S > NP + VP$. This tells us that the basic sentence type in English is made up of a noun phrase followed by a verb phrase. In order to get from a rule of this type to a sentence of the language, the grammar must interact with the lexicon. This is an ordered inventory of all the words in the language, including information about meaning and word class. Like the rules of grammar, the lexicon exists in the mind of the speaker; it forms the other necessary component of a language. NP and VP are variables; they specify that any phrase of the relevant type can fill this slot. NP can be replaced by actual phrases such as *the boy* and *the cat*, and VP by phrases such as *ran quickly* and *chased the dog*. Note that in this version of grammar the constituent VP contains the verb and everything that belongs with it, or complements it. This is different from definitions of VP you may come across in other accounts of grammar, including that used in *Discovering Language* (Jeffries, 2006), which uses VP to describe only the verbal component of the clause. This highlights the fact we considered in Chapter 1: that even apparently straightforward descriptions of language are often based on decisions by the linguist, and that different decisions can lead to different descriptions.

So the simple rule of sentence formation is capable of generating intransitive sentences such as *The boy ran quickly* and transitive sentences such as *The cat chased the dog*. There are of course other rules of this type. These include rules specifying the ways in which phrases such as noun phrases and verb phrases are themselves made up by combinations of individual words from different specific categories.

Rules of this type are referred to as phrase structure rules. In the examples we have just considered, a single rule explains how a huge variety of sentences of English are structured from individual components, or phrases. But these are not the only type of rules that form part of linguistic competence. Phrase structure rules are not in themselves sufficient to generate all the possible sentences of any human language. In particular they are not always very good at explaining what speakers of a language know about the ways in which grammatical relationships affect meanings. This is explained further in the following passage:

> We can distinguish the 'deep structure' of a sentence from its 'surface structure'. The former is the underlying abstract structure that determines its semantic interpretation; the latter, the superficial organization of units which determines the phonetic interpretation and which relates to the physical form of the actual utterance, to its perceived or intended form (Chomsky, 1966, p. 33).

What we would recognise as sentences of our language, including information about how they will sound if spoken, are the surface structures produced by the grammar. These are related to, but may be different from, the deep structures, which exist only in the minds of speakers and specify meaning. Surface structures are derived from deep structures by the application of a different type of rule, known as transformational rules. Chomskyan grammar is sometimes referred to as transformational-generative grammar.

To many, Chomsky's idea that grammar involves two different levels of structure and two different types of rule makes his account of language unnecessarily, indeed unfeasibly, complicated. His description of surface structure as superficial seems to miss the point: surface structures are what we encounter when we come into contact with language so they must surely be highly important. Chomsky's arguments in favour of his system rest chiefly on the complexity of the structures of language. He argues that once you start to look at the set of sentences of any language and the different possibilities of combination and meaning that make them up, you have no option but to describe them using a system as complex as the one he proposes. Having described the nature of surface structures he argues that:

> It is clear, however, that the deep structure must be quite different from this surface structure. For one thing, the surface representation in no way expresses the grammatical relations that are . . . crucial for semantic interpretation. Secondly, in the case of an ambiguous sentence such as, for example, (5), only a single surface structure may be assigned, but the deep structures must obviously differ (Chomsky, 1971, p. 78).

Chomsky's first point here is that the way in which speakers interpret sentences points to subtleties in grammatical relations that cannot be captured simply by specifying how sentences are built up by adding together phrases of different types. Sometimes surface structure masks the complexity of meaning, or obscures the ways in which apparently very similar sentences express very different ideas. Examples that Chomsky has used in his writings to support this claim, and that are frequently repeated in discussions of deep and surface structure are the pair of sentences *John is easy to please* and *John is eager to please*. These look very similar to each other, in terms of both the words they contain and how these words are grouped together. Each consists of a noun phrase *John*, followed by a verb phrase, *is*, and then an adjective phrase, either *easy to please* or *eager to please*. However, despite these apparent similarities in grammatical structure, speakers of English will recognise a huge difference in meaning between the two. In the first example *John* is the unspoken object of the verb *to please*; the sentence could be paraphrased as *It is easy to please John*. The second sentence cannot be paraphrased as *It is eager to please John*. In this case *John* is not the object of *to please* but the one doing the pleasing; in effect he is the hidden subject of *to please*. A more satisfactory paraphrase of this sentence would be *John is eager to please someone/everyone*.

Chomsky claims that the dramatically different meanings of these two examples must reflect significant differences between their deep structures, the level at which semantic relationships between the elements of a sentence are specified. In deep structure *John* is the object of *to please* in the first sentence but the subject of the verb in the second. Transformational rules, including a rule that deletes constituents such as *John* that are repeated in deep structure, produce surface structures that are deceptively similar looking and obscure the actual grammatical differences between the two sentences. The unconscious knowledge of deep structure on the part of speakers ensure that the two sentences are always interpreted differently, despite the fact that transformational rules make them appear to have the same surface structure.

The second argument that Chomsky advances in favour of deep structures in the passage quoted above is connected to ambiguous sentences. The example that he refers to there, his example (5), is the following sentence: *What disturbed John was being disregarded by everyone*. This is just one of the many examples of sentences that can be interpreted in two ways. In one interpretation it is John who is being disregarded. In the other it is a particular issue (an issue that is disturbing John) that is being disregarded. Chomsky's response to this is to suggest that, as in the case of the examples discussed above, these two interpretations are the result of significant differences at the level of deep structure. The single surface structure is produced in the two instances by the operation of different transformational rules that have the effect of disguising the significant differences between the two interpretations. In fact the apparently single but ambiguous sentence represents two totally different sentences of the language, in that it can be produced in different ways from two totally different deep structures.

A further argument that Chomsky has advanced in favour of the existence of deep structure, although it is not mentioned in the passage quoted above, works the other way around. Sometimes differences in surface structure can mask close similarities in deep structure that reflect similarities in how speakers interpret those surface structures. The relationship between active and passive sentences provides some useful examples here. Earlier we considered the sentence *The boy chased the dog*. This active sentence is very different in appearance, word order and indeed how it is structured into phrases, from the passive sentence *The dog was chased by the boy*. Yet part of knowing English is knowing that these two sentences are very similar in meaning; in sofar as they can be used to describe the same event they might be said to have the same meaning. In transformational-generative grammar the two sentences share the same deep structure, which explains this sameness of meaning. Different transformational rules operate on this deep structure to produce the active and the passive sentences that appear at surface structure. In this case the transformations obscure similarities rather than differences in deep structure.

We have looked here at a very brief outline of transformational-generative grammar: just enough to be able to understand what type of view Chomsky has taken of language and how this has affected what he thinks should be said about it. We have not really looked into the complexities of the grammar itself. And we have discussed transformational-generative grammar as though it were a single, static theory. This is very far from the case. Many different rules and grammars have been proposed and developed within the general framework of transformational-generative grammar. Chomsky himself has changed and modified his ideas over time. For instance in works written later than the passages we have considered here (for example Chomsky, 1981) he used the terms D structure and S structure instead of deep structure and surface structure, distancing himself from the notion of superficiality he originally associated with the latter. Also in later writings he concentrated on X-bar theory, a development of transformational-generative grammar that deals in common features of the structures of all phrase types and sentences. The 'minimalist program' (Chomsky, 1995) is an even more recent development that for many linguists is associated with Chomsky's current views on language. The emphasis of this is on the simplicity of rules and descriptions.

Chomsky's views on the role of theory in language study and on its relationship to data are easy to infer from his ideas about language itself. Most importantly he does not restrict his account of language to what can be observed. In this his approach is in complete opposition to the empiricism of, for instance, Bloomfield (1935), who insisted that descriptions of language could be made only inductively from observations. Chomsky's account of language includes many things that cannot be directly observed, or indeed proved empirically, including the generative and transformational rules of grammar, deep structures in the minds of speakers, and the innate language faculty. In fact these unempirical phenomena represent the most important features of Chomsky's account of language. As we saw in Section 1.2, Chomsky has argued that any theory that has something interesting to say must go beyond what is observable. The best theory will not merely describe the data but will offer an explanation of why it is as it is.

For those who argue that the best type of theory is an empirical one based only on what can be observed, the fact that Chomsky's linguistics relies on many phenomena that cannot be proved to exist constitutes a severe weakness. His approach, of course, is deductive rather than inductive. His theories are not just generalisations from data; they are hypotheses about what cannot be observed inspired by a desire to explain what can be observed. They are speculative but, he claims, falsifiable. No definite proof can be found for the existence of Universal Grammar, but it is possible to specify what sort of data would falsify that hypothesis. If a human language were to come to light that did not conform to any of the regularities of Universal Grammar so far identified, this would be enough to force the theory to be significantly modified or perhaps even abandoned. Chomsky and his followers claim that no such language has yet been found. Similarly the innateness hypothesis (IH) can never be conclusively proved. But it predicts that there will never be a human child with no physical or mental impairment who grows up in an environment where a human language is spoken yet fails to acquire that language successfully. The fact that all children learn a language is of course not sufficient to prove Chomsky's case. The IH is not the only possible explanation for this fact. But an exception to the rule would present a very strong challenge to the IH. Again, Chomsky's followers claim that no such exception has been identified.

Because of his speculative and mentalist – as opposed to generalising and materialist – approach to language study, Chomsky's work has sometimes been labelled 'rationalist'. Indeed he himself uses this description of his ideas. This label draws on the philosophical tradition of rationalism, in which properties of the human mind and mental processes are the main focus of inquiry. Rationalism is often discussed in opposition to empiricism; the latter tends to reject explanations that make reference to mental phenomena because these are not available for observation. However Chomsky is not averse to describing what he does as empirical, or even to claiming that his is the true empirical approach to language. In the following sentence he is describing the process of deducing properties of the language acquisition device (LAD), or the innate features of mind that allow language acquisition to take place. He argues that the linguist must draw on observations about the linguistic evidence available to the child, and the complexity of the language the child develops: 'Notice that this is an entirely empirical matter; there is no place for any dogmatic or arbitrary assumptions about the intrinsic, innate structure of the [LAD]' (Chomsky, 1968, p. 122).

For anyone who takes a simplistic view of the distinction between rationalism and empiricism, Chomsky's claim to empirical credentials might be very surprising. His point is that speculative deductive claims, for instance those about the existence and nature of a mental predisposition to acquire language, must be grounded in and tested against empirical observation. Deductive hypotheses may go beyond generalisations from data, but they are still bound by the available data. They must not be dogmatic, or unamenable to revision or abandonment in the face of the data. Nor should they be arbitrary; there must be a sound observational basis for whatever speculative claim is made. Chomsky has even claimed that 'The behavior of the speaker, listener, and learner of language constitutes, of course, the actual data for any study of language' (Chomsky, 1959, p. 56). Admittedly this was written early in Chomsky's career, when he was perhaps more ready than he would be later to acknowledge the importance to the linguist of the observable phenomena of language use. The point remains, however, that for Chomsky theories about language may be speculative and may refer to entities that can never be observed, but they start from, and make predictions that can be tested against, empirical evidence.

It is almost impossible to exaggerate the impact that Chomsky's work has had on linguistics since he first began to publish his ideas in the mid-twentieth century. Many linguists have been convinced that his is the best way to think about language, and have studied different languages, or different aspects of language, from this point of view. But many other linguists have been equally convinced that his ideas about language are mistaken and that the conclusions he has drawn from them are erroneous. In fact a substantial proportion of Chomsky's influence within linguistics has come about from linguists reacting against his understanding of what language is. We will consider to some of these reactions in the next section. In particular we will discuss the ideas of thinkers who have taken issue with Chomsky's dismissal of performance as relatively unimportant, and have argued that communication is an essential, in fact the defining, property of language.

One area of linguistics where Chomsky's influence has been particularly significant, in terms of both positive support for and reaction against, is the field of language acquisition. While Chomsky has not engaged in the study of children's language, or of the processes of language learning, his ideas about the nature of language in general, and specifically his innateness hypotheses, have some very significant implications for the processes that children go through when they learn a first language. We will therefore be returning to Chomsky's work again in Chapter 9 when we consider the question of how children learn language.

2.3   Language is communication

The idea that language should be explained in relation to communication has been around for a long time. This is hardly surprising; there is a strong common-sense appeal to this approach. We are probably most aware of language when we are sharing our thoughts with other people, or interpreting what they are saying to us. Our experience of language is so strongly linked to the ways in which we communicate with each other using language that it may not seem to make much sense to talk about one without the other. As we will see in this section, some theorists have gone further than this and argued that it makes no sense to draw a distinction between language and the use of language; language simply is a form of communication, and the only sensible way to discuss language is to discuss communication.

We saw some elements of these ideas earlier in this chapter when we looked at behaviourism. The theory that language should be defined by the ways in which people behave when they interact with each other, and that this definition should include the consequences of that behaviour, can be seen as one take on the notion of language as communication. But versions of 'language is communication' can be found much earlier than the twentieth century. For instance in 1690 the philosopher John Locke defined language as a means of representing ideas, 'whereby they might be made known to others, and the thoughts of men's minds be conveyed from one to another' (Locke, 1993, p. 225). According to this definition, the whole point of language is to communicate ideas among people. Note, though, that in Locke's definition there is room for 'thoughts' and 'minds'; he does not limit himself to observable phenomena. Defining language in terms of communication does not, or does not necessarily, mean defining it exclusively in terms of observable behaviour.

Although these ideas have been around for a long time, in more recent discussions they are often positioned in opposition to Chomskyan linguistics. It is not hard to spot why this might be. Chomsky's mentalist approach to language is concerned primarily with what goes on in the mind of an individual who knows a language. It concentrates on the competence of the individual speaker rather than on performance, which is of course where communication takes place. Indeed the distinction between competence and performance, so central to Chomskyan linguistics, is at best suspect to those who maintain that language is communication. It assumes that it is legitimate to discuss language in isolation and as something separate from its use in communication. Worst of all, Chomsky has explicitly dismissed the communicative use of language as being of marginal or, at his most extreme, of no interest to the linguist. Add to this the strength of Chomsky's influence on linguistics and the near total dominance that the Chomskyan approach is perceived to have in some areas, and the force of the reaction by those who want to maintain the importance of communication makes sense.

In this section we will largely concentrate on reactions to Chomsky's work and the approaches that have been proposed in opposition to it. There is no intention of putting a negative slant on these approaches by labelling them 'not Chomskyan'. Nor is it intended to give more prominence to Chomsky by defining other linguistic schools of thought, as well as his own, in relation to him. Rather it is a helpful way of looking at the relevant underlying assumptions about language. The theoretical commitment to and attitudes towards the subject matter of linguistics that accompany the view that language is communication can be seen most clearly when contrasted with those who hold the view that language is a state of mind.

The following passage from a work by the linguist Geoffrey Leech is typical of responses to Chomsky's work in the latter part of the twentieth century:

> A defect of this theory is that it cannot handle social facts about language; and a further defect is that in consequence, it cannot generalize linguistic descriptions beyond the linguistic competence of the individual. This difficulty has been disguised by Chomsky's claim to be dealing with the knowledge of the 'ideal native speaker-hearer' – an abstract and fictional version of the individual (Leech, 1983, p. 54).

The 'social facts about language' that Leech mentions are often central to criticisms of Chomsky. The ways in which people communicate using language, the differences between forms of linguistic communication in different cultures or societies, and the relationships between language and other forms of human activity, are all potential areas of interest to linguists, and are all ruled out of consideration in Chomskyan linguistics. However hard mentalist linguists study the competence of the individual they will not be able to use their findings to learn anything about these things. For Chomsky, of course, this is not a problem and does not signify a weakness in his theory. Competence is an abstract system that is the proper focus of linguistic research and is not affected by any social features coincidental to language use. For Leech and many other linguists, such claims can serve to disguise a serious deficiency: the social facts of language are real and important, and they ought to be discussed in linguistics.

This difference of opinion between Leech and Chomsky raises an important point about the types of disagreement we are dealing with in this chapter, and indeed in the subject matter of this book in general. This is something that we have touched on before, but it is worth reminding ourselves of it here: many of the differences and disputes that arise within linguistics are, quite simply, irresolvable. The opposing views stem from different assumptions about language. Those linguists who see language as a state of mind are not going to agree with Leech, and those who view it as communication are not going to agree with Chomsky; short of a complete about-turn on this fundamental point, no amount of persuasion or argument will make any difference. This is not a flaw in linguistics. Indeed one of the sources of fascination in language as an object of study is that it is complex and subtle enough to accommodate such radically different approaches.

It is also an historical fact that linguistics has developed out of a number of disciplines. Different branches of linguistics have their origins in different fields of study, so it is hardly surprising that they are built on different assumptions about what they are studying. For instance in 1970s the anthropological linguist Dell Hymes complained that under Chomsky's influence linguistics was 'veering from its roots in anthropology' (Hymes, 1974, p. ix). For Hymes the loss of interest in communication and the social functions of language was not just a weakness in linguistics, it was a betrayal of its origins in anthropology, a discipline that focuses on just such aspects of human beings. Chomskyan linguists would not recognise either the weakness or the betrayal. As we saw in the previous section they work in a tradition that draws on a rationalist philosophy. Philosophical studies of language have not traditionally taken social and interactive factors as their focus of study, but rather mental and logical ones.

Hymes is credited with laying the foundations for the ethnography of communication, an approach to language study that draws heavily on anthropology and seeks to explain communication in relation to social and cultural settings. In some ways it is similar in aim and method to sociolinguistics, which we considered in Chapter 1. Sociolinguistics is another field that might be said to take as its starting point the belief that language is communication. As we will see, these are not the only branches of linguistics that concentrate on the communicative aspect of language. There are a variety of approaches to language – many of which have been developed relatively recently – that fall into this general category. They differ in terms of their particular focus on aspects of communication, the methodology they use and their views on the relationship between theory and data.

One thing that all these approaches have in common. however, is that they reject Chomsky's claim that the intuitions of a native speaker are the most appropriate data for linguists to work with. This is hardly surprising, because of course it follows from differences of opinion about the importance of performance. Competence is the primary focus of study for the Chomskyan linguist. As a mental phenomenon it is not available for immediate inspection, so a speaker's judgments about the sentences produced by that competence are the best sources of evidence available. In effect linguists who are interested in communication focus on performance. Finding out about competence does not tell us about performance, or at least tells us very little about it. There are a whole host of other factors, including social and contextual situations and factors that Chomsky would dismiss as performance errors, that need to be considered by those who view language as communication. Indeed many of the linguists who do not recognise a distinction between language and the use of language view competence as an artificial construction. Far from being the true location of human language, it is the product of attempts to tidy up examples of language by removing messy and inconvenient features of context and social situation. William Labov, who is viewed by many as the founder of sociolinguistics, wrote forcefully that 'either our theories are about the language that ordinary people use on the street, arguing with friends, or at home blaming their children, or they are about very little indeed' (Labov, 1972, p. 109).

In contrast to Chomskyan linguists, then, those who view language as communication put a high value on authentic data as the basis of their research. The nature of this data varies between disciplines. It can be evidence of naturally occurring conversations that have been recorded and then transcribed for the purposes of study. It can be written texts that were produced for communicative purposes outside of linguistics but are then collected for linguistic analysis. In the case of sociolinguistics it can be the results of interviews with speakers of a particular language or language variety. These speakers are not asked to make grammaticality judgments, but are questioned about their attitudes towards the language or their pronunciation of particular words. The sociolinguist would ideally compare the answers to these questions with evidence about how the same speakers actually behave linguistically in spontaneous conversation. In all cases the approach is empirical; data is collected and analysed so that the researcher can find out something about communication, and therefore about language.

The idea that language is best seen in its full social context and studied by observation, rather than in isolation and studied by intuition, has not arisen simply as a response to Chomsky. When sociolinguists and linguists working in other branches of linguistics wanted to respond to Chomsky there was already a body of work upon which they could draw. In 1935 the linguist J. R. Firth wrote that 'Neither linguists nor psychologists have begun the study of conversation; but it is here we shall find the key to a better understanding of what language really is and how it works' (Firth, 1935, p. 32). More than two decades before Chomsky began publishing his ideas about competence and performance, Firth was suggesting that language existed primarily in the ways in which people communicated with each other, and therefore studying language meant studying those processes of communication. Note that he did not advocate the study of conversation in order to learn about the use of language, but to learn about language itself: about what it is. Some years later he wrote:

> The linguist studies the speaking person in the social process. It has been said that two persons taking part in the continuity of repetitions in the social process offer material for most branches of linguistics in making statements of meaning (Firth, 1951, p. 190).

The material to which Firth referred (the data necessary for linguistic study) was to be found in the interactions between two speakers of a language. Crucially it included 'the social process', or speakers interacting with each other within a society. Some of the more hostile criticisms of Chomsky have hinted or argued explicitly that by studying language in isolation from communication, hence ignoring the social process, he is in effect not living in the real world. The following passage from a late-twentieth-century commentator on language is typical:

> Chomsky's theory does not profess to be about the real world of variant forms which real-life speakers actually use. Rather, it is entirely based on the theoretical model of the 'ideal' speaker-listener in an (imaginary) completely homogeneous speech community, of a kind which we all know exists nowhere, but which is conjured up in order to develop rules about the supposed 'underlying' grammar which every speaker possesses (Honey, 1997, p. 45).

Words such as 'imaginary', 'conjured up' and 'supposed' are highly emotive and designed to put Chomsky's ideas in a bad light. Nevertheless Honey does present a fairly accurate picture of Chomkyan linguistics; he just makes it clear that he does not see it as the correct approach. The 'ideal speaker-listener' does not actually exist but is a theoretical construct that allows us to say something about the central feature of language: the competence of a native speaker. This notion is perhaps the most controversial aspect of Chomskyan linguistics. For some commentators the choice of the word ideal is particularly unfortunate. As we saw in the previous section, the ideal that Chomsky is interested in is an entirely theoretical one. But some linguists have picked up on the social or even the moral overtones sometimes associated with the word. When we looked at the work of Roy Harris in Section 2.1

we saw that he rejects what he calls segregationist approaches to linguistics that isolate language from other facts about human behaviour and social interaction. Perhaps predictably, he is not impressed by Chomskyan linguistics. But he even goes so far as to claim that Chomsky treats competence as 'an ideal towards which our imperfect systems of human communication should aspire, or in terms of which they can and should be described' (Harris, 1996, p. 164).

Not all criticisms of Chomsky's reduction of linguistics to the study of mental competence are quite so scathing. We looked earlier at Dell Hymes' complaint that linguistics was losing sight of its roots in anthropology, and we will consider some of Hymes' ideas in a little more detail here. They are representative of the outlook of the ethnography of communication, and in many important respects of sociolinguistics too. The goals to which Hymes refers in the following passage include that of describing linguistic competence, and specifically of describing it in such a way as to explain linguistic creativity.

> I share Chomsky's goals for linguistics, and admire him for setting them, but they cannot be reached on his terms or by linguistics alone. Rules of appropriateness beyond grammar govern speech, and are acquired as part of conceptions of self, and of meanings associated both with particular forms of speech and with the act of speaking itself (Hymes, 1974, p. 94).

Hymes is pointing out that what is judged linguistically appropriate depends not just on the rules of the grammar but also on a raft of social, cultural and psychological factors to do with meaning and even personal identity. In other words, all the factors that for Chomsky are related only to performance must play a more central role in explaining language. For this reason, studying just the language system can never tell linguists everything they need to know about language. Hymes argues in more detail elsewhere that linguistics cannot and should not proceed in isolation from disciplines such as sociology, psychology and anthropology.

Hymes claims to admire and support Chomsky's goal of explaining competence. However the extra features that make up our ability to use language appropriately and that Hymes argues need to be accounted for go far beyond Chomsky's definition of competence. Hymes insists that linguists should concentrate on what he labels 'sociolinguistic competence' or 'communicative competence' as much as on a narrowly defined notion of linguistic competence. The model that he has devised to explain language includes features as diverse as setting, participants, purposes and agreements about social acceptability. These are of course all features of individual occasions of speech. For Hymes, to explain language is to explain what goes on in any occurrence of speech.

In terms of appropriate methodology for the study of language, it is not surprising that Hymes stresses the need to pay attention to real life examples. It is necessary not just to collect lots of examples of speech in order to study language, but also to be prepared to take account of individual occurrences. For instance he writes that he has heard the statement 'Tom looks after Tom', where the two occurrences of 'Tom' refer to the same person. Transformational-generative grammar would predict that this is not a possible sentence of the language because of what are known as 'binding conditions' on reference (Chomsky, 1981). Therefore presumably a Chomskyan linguist would dismiss this example as being affected by performance errors, rather than being evidence that it forms a part of the language. Hymes argues that it is not possible for grammarians to dismiss so lightly the things that people say in their actual speech. Since this example has been observed to occur, any account of language must be able to explain it. In a similar way he argues that linguists should pay attention to hesitations, false starts and the other features of the ways in which people express themselves in speech. Linguists whose main focus is mental competence would of course dismiss these as features of performance that are determined by factors such as memory, attention, tiredness and so on, and that are definitely not linguistic. For Hymes they occur as a normal part of speaking, so a description of speaking – that is, of language, must say something about them.

Hymes does not have much to say explicitly about the role of theory in language study. However he says enough for us to be able to understand what he views as the appropriate relationship between theory and data. In the following passage he is discussing the requirements of a theory of language:

> One needs fresh kinds of data, one needs to investigate directly the use of language in contexts of situation, so as to discern patterns proper to speech activity, patterns that escape separate studies of grammar, of personality, of social structure, religion, and the like, each abstracting from the patterning of speech activity into some other frame of reference (Hymes, 1974, pp. 3–4).

In this passage Hymes is emphasising, as we might expect, that linguists should look at language in context, and that what they are studying is 'speech activity' rather than language as an independent mental capacity. He is also arguing against the reductionism of concentrating on language in isolation from other aspects of human activity. A full study of speech activity would involve consideration of psychological, social and even religious phenomena. Note also that he refers to studying the data of speech activity in order to discern patterns that will form the basis of an appropriate theory of language. We can recognise in this the inductive scientific method, building up from observation to theory through generalisation. In this too Hymes can be contrasted with Chomsky, whose deductive approach is driven by the formation of theories that can then be tested against the available evidence for possible falsification.

Hymes is one of many linguists who have argued that reducing the study of language to the study of an autonomous mental competence means ignoring much of what is most interesting. As we have seen, the social, interactive and interpersonal features of communication are not studied in Chomskyan linguistics. But for many linguists these are the most interesting features, or are the most compelling reasons for studying language. Chomsky has also been criticised for absolving himself of social and political responsibility. There are many issues of inequality, discrimination and policy, for instance, that accompany communication but that can be ignored in the study of an abstract and isolated mental competence. For instance feminist linguists have considered how language can perpetuate or alternatively challenge prejudices and social norms. Here is one feminist commentary on Chomskyan linguistics:

> As it is concerned with language as an abstraction and tends to view actual production (performance) as typically flawed, and since it has little to say about how language produces meaning, interacts with our knowledge of the world or with social systems, it is not very useful for a person concerned with how language serves women, describes women or how women use language (Gibbon, 1999, pp. 19–20).

Critical discourse analysis is built on the belief that careful analysis of texts can reveal underlying belief systems and illuminate the ways in which the use of language is bound up with the maintenance and use of power in society. In his book on the relationship between language and power, Norman Fairclough (1989) criticises what he calls mainstream linguistics for its concentration on competence rather than actual language use. He argues that the study of language without regard for variation within communities and over time, together with the 'neglect of language practice', result in 'an idealized view of language, which isolates it from the social and historical matrix outside of which is cannot actually exist' (ibid., p. 7).

Critical discourse analysts, and indeed discourse analysts in general, tend to draw on the work of Michael Halliday in their approach to spoken or written text. Halliday, and in particular his 'functional grammar' (see Halliday, 1985), is sometimes discussed as the main alternative to Chomsky and formal grammar in late-twentieth-century linguistics. Formal grammar is concerned primarily with describing and explaining the patterns and regularities of a language: the different sentence structures that are possible and how they are related to each other syntactically. Functional grammar pays attention to and attempts to account for how language is used, or the functions that it serves. Halliday was not the first to look at language in these terms. He developed his functional grammar against a background of a history of functional approaches to language. Functional approaches are driven primarily by an interest in meaning and purpose rather than structure.

Halliday certainly does not ignore the patterns and regularities of language. The 'systemic functional grammar' that he has developed is designed to explain how the structures of the language are put together by speakers making choices from a series of options presented to them by the system. So for Halliday the system of language very definitely exists, and is in need of description and explanation. The system has taken on its form not arbitrarily, or because of abstract features of the human mind, but because of the uses to which language is put. The form of a language follows from and is determined by its functions. Form can certainly be discussed, but it cannot be discussed without function. To put it in terms with which we are more familiar, linguists can and indeed must study and describe language, but they cannot do so without studying and describing the use of language.

The relationship that Halliday posits between language and the use of language is extremely complex. In Chomskyan linguistics, as we have seen, the two are kept entirely separate and are viewed as dependent on different types of factor. Halliday's account of how the grammatical system of the language is put together includes information about how it will be used. He defines three 'metafunctions' for language, or three general purposes to which language is put, which are represented in the linguistic system. The first is the 'ideational' metafunction, which is concerned with how individuals make sense of their environment. We might think of this as the way in which we represent the world to ourselves. This is perhaps close to the primary purpose of language in Chomskyan linguistics: language as an instrument of thought. Centrally linguistic purposes do not end there for Halliday, however. He also includes 'interpersonal' metafunctions, which concern the purposes to which language is put. So social, interactive and communicative uses of language are brought into the structure of language. The third metafunction of language is the 'textual' one, which is concerned with how passages of language use are put together and how they are related to their contexts.

The text is an extremely important element of linguistic analysis and description in systemic functional linguistics. It is broadly defined to include any extended piece of language use, whether written or spoken. Textual analysis is part of the motivation for systemic functional grammar in a way that is not the case for transformational generative grammar. This reflects the fact that Halliday's interests are much more 'applied' than Chomsky's. Whereas Chomsky's interest has always been in finding out about language for its own sake, or for the insight it gives us into the human mind, Halliday is interested in the use of language in various social and, particularly, educational settings. His grammar has been used to analyse the language of textbooks, teacher–pupil interactions and children's written compositions, among many other text types.

Halliday argues that an adequate linguistic theory must be able to explain both the language system and the texts it produces. He accuses linguistics as a discipline of placing too much emphasis on the system as the location of language, at the expense of the text. Significantly he does not advocate abandoning the language system in order to focus exclusively on the text. His argument is that the two are so closely connected that the study of one makes no sense without the study of the other. Studying language must necessarily involve studying the use of language in texts; but at the same time:

> A text is meaningful because it is an actualization of the potential that constitutes the linguistic system; it is for this reason that the study of discourse ('text linguistics') cannot properly be separated from the study of the grammar that lies behind it (Halliday, 1985, p. 345).

Halliday's interest in texts is the source of two major differences from but also, perhaps surprisingly, one similarity to Chomskyan linguistics. The similarity lies in Halliday's references to the system as existing alongside but separately from the texts it produces. For Halliday, as for Chomsky, there is a distinction between the language system and the use of language. They do not see the distinction in the same way, however, and this is the source of the first major difference. For Halliday the text is just as much a part of the language as is the system. The system is utilised every time a text is produced. But the language consists in part of a collection of all such texts. It follows that every time a text is produced the language itself is affected, however slightly; the collection of texts that make up the language has changed. In Chomskyan linguistics a text can never alter the language. Language is a self-contained system, independent of and only coincidentally linked to any use to which it might be put when creating texts.

The second major difference between Halliday and Chomsky that is demonstrated by Halliday's concentration on texts is to do with the appropriate level of linguistic description. The most important level in Chomskyan linguistics is that of the sentence. The goal is to describe a grammar that will produce all the sentences of a language, and explain their structure. A language is a finite set of rules that produces an infinite set of sentences. The question of how and why those sentences are put together in texts is not one to be addressed by the linguist. All sorts of psychological, social and cultural factors might be at play when people join sentences to form texts of different types. These are not linguistic factors and therefore need not, indeed should not, be explained within the language. Halliday insists on the analysis and description of texts as a correct procedure for linguists. For him, texts as well as sentences can tell us about the language system. In other words language is not restricted to producing sentences that can then be combined into texts. The interpersonal and textual metafunctions that form parts of language ensure that the ways in which texts are put together are just as much a matter for linguists as the ways in which sentences are put together.

In systemic functional grammar, therefore, and in the different approaches to discourse analysis that follow from it, linguistic description is not restricted to the level of the sentence, but includes larger units of language use. Here is an account of this issue in a textbook on discourse analysis:

> Linguists have long been interested in the structure of words (morphology) and sentences (syntax). Discourse analysis has moved the description of structure up a level, looking at actual stretches of connected text or transcript and providing descriptions of the structure of paragraphs, stories and conversations (Johnstone, 2002, p. 5).

Discourse analysts generally select particular texts for investigation and analyse them in detail in relation to the structures mentioned above. Texts are often selected because they are interesting from an aesthetic, social or ideological point of view. Another text-based approach to language study is to compile collections of different texts and to look for patterns and general features among them. This is the approach taken in corpus linguistics. We considered the implications of corpus linguistics when we considered the relationship between theory and data, and we will end this chapter with a brief consideration of the views about language that it presumes, and the relationship of these to the other views we have examined.

A corpus is a large collection or body of texts that are brought together for the purpose of linguistic analysis. This used to be done manually, but nowadays the term corpus is nearly always short hand for electronic or machine-readable corpus. Bodies of texts are stored on computers and analysed using software such as concordancer programs, which compile lists of the occurrences of particular words in their textual contexts. Many argue that it is the development and availability of computers that has made corpus linguistics viable as a methodology. The corpus linguist can analyse quickly and accurately huge collections of both written texts and transcriptions of spoken texts.

Corpus linguists commonly claim that theirs is the best or the only reasonable approach to language study, because a corpus gives you access to 'real world language', or language as it really is rather than as theoretical linguists consider it to be. This claim is of course based on a very large assumption: that language is the body of instances of communication going on in the world, available for collection and analysis. According to corpus linguists, when you look at instances of communication you are looking at the language. It is therefore necessary to treat all texts in a corpus, and indeed all words in each text, as equally important for linguistic analysis. If someone has said or written something, the argument goes, then that must be part of the language and must be treated seriously by linguists. The view that a language is the collection of instances of how it is used in communication is apparent, for instance, in the following quotation from a textbook on corpus linguistics:

> It is now possible for researchers with access to a personal computer and off-the-shelf software to do linguistic analysis using a corpus, and to dis-cover facts about a language which have never been noticed or written about previously (Kennedy, 1998, p. 3).

Analysis of a corpus reveals facts about a language; the patterns of usage are where the language is located.

The alternative, less enthusiastic view of corpus linguistics is predicable enough. Chomskyan linguists argue that a corpus is not and can never be a source of facts about a language because it is no more than a list of occur-rences of uses of language. Analysis of a corpus will only ever be able to reveal facts about performance, never about underlying competence, and is there-fore of very limited interest to the linguist. Placing significance on individual instances of use or on a large collection of uses can be very misleading; the linguist may end up basing claims about language on little more than a series of performance errors. Furthermore, unlike intuitive judgments the corpus will not be able to tell linguists about combinations of words that speakers would not use because they are not grammatical sentences of the language. Nor will it be able to distinguish these from combinations that speakers would not use because they were socially unacceptable, or because they described unlikely or impossible situations. Worse still, whatever information a corpus can give about a language will be partial and incomplete. A natural language is infinite, while any corpus compiled for that language will neces-sarily be finite and therefore inadequate.

Corpus linguists have countered that the increasing size of corpora largely defeats the 'inadequate' argument. Corpora can be very large indeed, con-taining many millions of words. Although they necessarily remain finite, they can be constructed from a variety of text types and genres so as to be 'representative' of the language as a whole. They argue that the Chomskyan obsession with grammatical and ungrammatical strings is an artificial one; it is more interesting and instructive to look at what people actually say or write. Introspection may provide certain types of information about language, but it is no good as a source of quantitative data for linguists who want to compare frequencies of occurrence and perform statistical analyses of the language. Furthermore introspective data cannot be 'verified', in the sense that it cannot be checked by another researcher to confirm findings based on it, whereas a corpus is always available for objective scrutiny and the comparison of results. The argument that corpus analysis can only ever tell us about the vagaries of performance, never about underlying competence, cannot really be countered because it rests on a completely different set of assumptions from those that underpin corpus linguistics. To the corpus linguist, this argument makes no sense. It is artificial to claim that linguists ought to be studying something called 'language' that is distinct from the actualities of everyday communication.

As the above sketch of opposing views suggests, the differences between corpus linguists and mentalist linguists have been the subject of an extended debate. This has at times been heated, even acrimonious. Nowadays linguists on both sides are in general less interested in taking swipes at each other's methodologies. Some have even started to think about ways in which the two approaches might complement each other. The following discussion of the issue is from a recent overview of corpus linguistics:

> The division and divisiveness that has characterized the relationship between the corpus linguist and the generative grammarian rests on a false assumption: that all corpus linguists are descriptivists, interested only in counting and categorizing constructions occurring in a corpus, and that all generative grammarians are theoreticians unconcerned with the data on which their theories are based. Many corpus linguists are actively engaged in issues of language theory, and many generative grammarians have shown an increasing concern for the data on which their theories are based, even though data collection remains at best a marginal concern in modern generative theory (Meyer, 2002, p. 1).

Meyer is suggesting here that nowadays corpus linguists are interested not just in describing patterns among the data in their corpora, but in going beyond these to make more general observations about the language. It is possible to go further than this, and to note that corpus linguists are now often keen to point out that a corpus does not give unimpeded access to facts about the language. In order to analyse a corpus, linguists make decisions about what features to look at and how to interpret the results; they are necessarily imposing certain assumptions on the data. This is even more marked when corpora are 'tagged'; in other words, when information is included about the grammatical word classes in a text. This can be very useful as a tool for searching a corpus to find out about grammatical constructions and possible combinations, but it is achieved at the expense of the objective nature of the data and it remains a controversial procedure in the field of corpus linguistics. Meyer also suggests, although perhaps more reservedly, that some linguists in the Chomskyan tradition are willing to consider the possibility of using corpus data to test out linguistic hypotheses.

One particularly enthusiastic advocate of corpus linguistics is Geoffrey Sampson. We looked briefly at Sampson's attitude towards language in Section 2.1, where we saw that he defined it very explicitly as an aspect of human behaviour, to be investigated by observation. It is no surprise, then, that Sampson vehemently rejects intuition as a legitimate source of linguistic data. Instead he argues that linguists must use empirical methods, which nowadays means using corpora. Corpus linguistics, he suggests, should not be seen as a specialist branch of linguistics:

> To be a corpus linguist is simply to be an empirical linguist, making appropriate use of the available tools and resources which are enabling linguists at the turn of the century to discover more than their predecessors were able to discover, when empirical techniques were last in vogue (Sampson, 2001, p. 6).

Here Sampson is making it quite clear that he sees corpus linguistics as belonging to, or as a simple continuation of, the tradition of empirical linguistics. Corpora make the investigation of language by means of observation of data easier than it was for linguists such as Bloomfield, so it makes sense to use them. Any piece of data that appears in a corpus is appropriate subject matter for the linguist because 'empirical linguistics has to deal with everything that is out there' (ibid., p. 8).

This claim really goes to the heart of the issues we have been focusing on in this section: the implications of the belief that language is communication, and how these differ from the implications of the belief that language is a state of mind. If language is the collection of ways in which people communicate with each other linguistically, then it really is 'out there' to be observed and studied. That is, language exists in the world around us, in the interactions we observe in our daily lives. For the mentalist linguist, in contrast, language might be said to be 'in here'; it exists in the mind of the individual speaker. The observable phenomena of communication depend not only on language but also on many other factors, so they are not a very reliable source of evidence about language. Certainly, not too much store should be set by one occurrence of language use that has been collected in a corpus, or even by a number of such occurrences. They might well have been the product of lapses in concentration, of confusion or of distraction. What is out there can be misleading and should be treated with caution.

It might look as though empirical linguists and mentalist linguists are at an impasse: a disagreement that cannot be resolved and from which there is apparently no way out. Impasses do not come much bigger than this one; there is disagreement not just about how best to study the subject matter, which is bad enough, but even about what the subject matter actually is. But a more optimistic way of looking at things is to say that the irresolvable differences do not matter because each approach can tell us about different aspects of language, even different aspects of what it is to be a human being. Some linguists still spend a lot of time arguing for the supremacy of their way of doing things, but others have come round to this more optimistic way of thinking. The linguist Frederick Newmeyer has suggested that 'the field of linguistics certainly has enough room to embrace both orientations' (Newmeyer, 1986, p. 133).

Certainly all the different approaches to language we have considered here have some interesting things to tell us. In Part II we will look at some questions that might occur to anyone who starts thinking about language, but for which we can only really find answers by looking at linguistics. There are generally a number of different possible answers to each of these questions. As we will see, these answers are based on various decisions that theorists have made about language, including how best to define and study it.

2.4   Further reading

Jeffries (2006) provides an overview of the conventional divisions of present-day linguistics into different branches. In particular see Section 1.5.3 of that volume for more on the notion of the linguistic 'sign', which we have considered in relation to integrationism; Section 1.5.1 for the distinction between 'competence' and 'performance', which is central to Chomsky's work; Section 5.7.2 for more on active and passive sentences, which we have considered in relation to Chomsky's views on deep structure; and Section 7.4.2 for Halliday's metafunctions.

Clark (2006) discusses the specific methods and terminologies of the approaches that can be said to share, to varying degrees, the assumption that language is communication. See in particular Chapter 2 for a more detailed discussion of pragmatics; Section 2.2 for the ethnography of communication; and Chapter 4 for more on critical discourse analysis. The whole book, and especially Chapter 2, is concerned with the role of 'authentic data' in language study.

Applying Language Theory

Introduction to Part II

In Part I we considered some of the main issues relevant to the ways in which linguists and philosophers have thought about language over the centuries and up to the present day. In particular we looked at three different broad definitions of what language is, and at how these have affected what has been said about language and how it has been studied. In Part II we are turning our attention to some more specific questions. These are the sorts of questions that might occur to anyone who starts thinking about language, and they are also questions that have been the subject of much discussion by professional theorists of language. The more general ideas from Part I are still highly relevant here. As we will see, the specific and sometimes competing answers that have been suggested to these questions can often be shown to be based on different assumptions about the best way in which to define language. In other words, the chapters in this section introduce some of the ways in which the general theories we have considered can be applied to answering specific questions about language.

How do Words Work?

3.1 Introduction

How words work is one of the most fundamental and important questions that we are likely to come across when we are thinking about language, but it is also one of the most easily overlooked. Whatever view of language we take, we need to be able to explain the fact that collections of speech sounds or marks on a piece of paper can relate to the things, experiences and qualities in the world around us. The fact that such an important question is easily overlooked is a result of the everyday nature of language, which can often get in the way when we try thinking about it seriously. As individuals we have been relating words to objects and properties since before we can remember, and have become so used to doing so that we feel no need to stop and question how that relationship works. When we are encouraging a baby to start using language we tell her the names of things around her. If she reaches for her cup we might say 'juice', or 'that's called juice'. We do not stop to worry about what we are doing by associating the word with the object, or what it means to say that an object is called something, or has a name.

One type of occasion that brings us close to the question of how words work is when someone challenges us to define or explain a word we have used. In the case of words that refer to complicated or abstract ideas, it is often easiest to do this by offering a definition of the word in question. For example we can say that '*ophiology* is the study of snakes' or that '*rhopalic* means that each word in a verse is one syllable longer than the word before'. This is a very useful way of explaining individual word meanings, but of course it does not take us any further towards answering the question of how words work in the first place, because we are simply defining one word by replacing it with a number of other words. For simpler words, particularly those relating to objects around us, we may find it easier to point. If there is one nearby at the time, we might point to a particular type of picture and say 'That's a *lithograph*' or even 'This is what *lithograph* means'. In doing so, and without thinking too much about it, we are adopting what has become known as a direct reference account of meaning. We are in effect saying that the meaning of the word lithograph is simply the object, the actual physical thing, to which it refers. The direct reference account of meaning is certainly intuitively appealing, and it has been much discussed over the years, but as we will see it brings with it its own problems.

3.2   Direct reference

The direct reference account of meaning is most commonly discussed in connection with nouns, for reasons that are obvious. It is much easier to point at something and say 'That's what *apple* means', 'That's what *tree* means' or 'That's what *aardvark* means' than it is to point at an instance of *thoughtful* or *deceive*. But in principle it is possible to extend the direct reference account to any word we want to define, if we allow that the reference of a word can be a thing or a property or an action. In each case there is something in the world of human experience, something that we learn about through our interactions with our environment, that is directly labelled by the word in question.

The thing or property that the word refers to is sometimes described as the 'extension' of the word. So the direct reference account is an extensional account of meaning, in that it explains meaning entirely in relation to the world outside language. The meaning of a word is simply its extension in the world. This raises the first problem with the direct reference account of meaning. There are words in our language that do not have extensions in the world. To see this we only have to think of fairy tales or myths. *Troll, dragon, leprechaun* and *mermaid* are all words that, according to present-day understanding, have no extension in the real world. But we would hardly want to say that because of this the words are meaningless, and demand that all fairy tales be scrapped immediately because they contain words that have no meaning. If a purely extensional account of meaning were correct we would be completely at a loss to explain the meaning of such words. And things get even worse for the direct reference account of meaning when we try to explain proper names.

Proper names such as *Elizabeth II, London, Disneyland* and *Frank Sinatra* are an important part of language, and as such they need to be explained by an account of how words work. They are crucially different from the types of word we have considered so far because they relate to just one individual or place. In our earlier example, when we pointed at a picture and said 'This is what *lithograph* means' we were of course cheating slightly. The word lithograph does not act as a label for just one thing in the world, so to give the full meaning of the word we would have to point at everything that can be described as a lithograph. It is just that it is not normally practical to point to more than a handful of objects when defining a word in this way. In other words, the extension of the word lithograph is the set of all the objects in the world that we might describe as being a lithograph. Similarly the extensions of *apple, tree* and *aardvark* are large groups of individual objects. One consequence of this is that the actual extension of most words is changing all the time. Even as you are reading this, some apples, trees and aardvarks are just coming into being, replacing other older examples. In the case of a proper name, however, there is generally only one object acting as its extension. At first glance this makes the direct reference account particularly appealing as a description of proper names: 'You want to know the meaning of *Elizabeth II*? Go along to The Trooping of the Colour and you can have a look at her'; 'What does *London* mean? Here's a train ticket so you can go and see for yourself'.

However if the meaning of a proper name were simply the individual referred to, we would be at a loss to explain the fact that some individuals have more than one name. This is frequently the case when people have a name that is related to their official position. For instance, as well as being Elizabeth II, that particular individual has her own personal name: Elizabeth Alexandra Mary Windsor. A straightforward direct reference account would have to say that these two names are exact synonyms; they share the same extension in the world so there is no difference between them in terms of meaning. The situation is even more puzzling when we describe an individual rather than simply naming him or her. If our account of meaning is purely extensional, then the meaning of an entire noun phrase such as *the Queen of England* can be no more than the particular individual in the world – in this case the same individual who is the meaning of *Elizabeth II*. So phrases such as *the most successful pop star in the world, the best selling fiction writer of all time* and *the inventor of Miss Marple* should mean no more and no less than the proper names of the individuals in question. Furthermore, if the last two phrases happen to refer to the same person they have to be exactly equivalent in meaning. Yet intuitively these conclusions seem unacceptable; there are significant differences in meaning between *Elizabeth II* and *Elizabeth Alexandra Mary Windsor*, and between *the best selling fiction writer of all time* and *the inventor of Miss Marple*. It was in response to problems like this that some rather elaborate accounts of how words work have been developed. We will consider one of these next.

3.3 Focus on Frege

Gottlob Frege was a German mathematician who lived in the late nineteenth and early twentieth centuries. He produced a lot of highly technical work that has been significant in the development of present-day mathematics and logic. However in the area of language theory he is known mainly because of one article in which he addressed the problems with meaning that we have just been considering. It was not a complete change of direction for Frege to take an interest in meaning. He thought that it was necessary to understand how language worked before it could properly be used as a tool for discussing logic. In Frege's eyes, natural language was messy and imperfect in comparison with the artificial languages of mathematics and logic. Before it could be of any use to him he needed to understand language so that he could tidy it up and get rid of its unfortunate imperfections. Despite this rather dismissive attitude, later theorists have found his ideas valuable in discussions of language for its own sake.

Frege approached the problem of meaning in connection with so-called 'identity statements'. These had been discussed in logic for some time and Frege proposed a new theory of meaning to explain them. An identity statement is a sentence in which a single individual is identified in two different ways; we could say that two different names or descriptions that refer to the same individual are brought together. An example would be: *London is the capital of England*. This might look like a perfectly straightforward sentence, the sort of thing that turns up in everyday use without causing any problems. And in a sense that is just the point. We use sentences like this all the time, but if the simple direct reference account of meaning were correct they would be unacceptable to anyone with an interest in logic.

To understand why identity statements present logical problems we need to think about what they tell us about an individual. If the meaning of a proper name such as *London* and a descriptive phrase such as *the capital of England* were simply what is referred to, the city situated on the banks of the River Thames, then the identity statement in question simply picks out an individual and tells us that it is identical to itself. In other words, if the meaning of a word or phrase is its extension, then *London is the capital of England* should mean exactly the same as *London is London*. To use the logical notation that Frege favoured, the logical meaning of our identity statement ought to be $x = x$. The letter x is what is known as a variable. It takes the place of any entity of some particular type that we care to name: in this case, any way of identifying an individual. The logical $x = x$ equation is completely uninformative – although true, it is hardly news to be told that an entity is the same as itself.

Natural language identity statements, on the other hand, can be both true and informative. They can be used to tell people something about the world that they did not already know and could not have worked out for themselves.

In order to explain this apparent paradox, Frege suggested that we need to think of words as having two types of meaning. All words and phrases have both these types of meaning. Firstly, there is the actual entity referred to. Frege's German word for this type of meaning, *Bedeutung*, has variously been translated as 'meaning', 'reference' and 'denotation', among other possibilities. So Frege's new version of meaning included the direct reference account; *Bedeutung* describes the extension of a word or phrase, or the actual thing to which it refers. But for Frege the direct reference account by itself was not sufficient to explain how words work. As well as extensional meaning, all words and phrases have what is sometimes now described in language theory as 'intensional meaning'. Frege's original word, *Sinn*, is usually translated as 'sense'. The sense of a word or phrase is the means by which it picks out an individual in the world, or the way in which the reference is identified. So *London* and *the capital of England* share the same reference; they both have the same actual city as their extension. But they are not exactly equivalent in meaning because although they have the same reference they have totally different senses. They each use a different method to identify the city in question: the former by using its proper name, the latter by providing an identifying description of it.

Once we allow that words have senses as well as references, identity statements no longer present a problem. We no longer have to see them as having the uninformative meaning $x = x$, because we are not restricted to describing them in terms of extensional meaning. When words are used it is sometimes their reference that is most significant and sometimes it is their sense. If you say *I am going to London tomorrow*, then what is important is the reference of the word *London*. If you say *London is the capital of England*, then what is important is the sense of *London*. You are not saying of a single entity that it is identical to itself. You are saying of two different sets of words that they share the same reference.

Frege argued that, as well as explaining the apparent problem posed by statements of identity, his distinction between sense and reference solved another long-standing logical puzzle: the existence of so-called 'opaque contexts'. In most cases, if there are two words or phrases that are extensionally equivalent it is possible to swap them for each other in any context without altering the truth of a statement. 'Context' here refers to the immediate linguistic context provided by the sentence in which a word occurs. For instance, if we can agree that *Neil Armstrong* and *the first man to set foot on the moon* are extensionally equivalent, then swapping one for the other in a variety of contexts should make no difference to truth. Since *Neil Armstrong is American* is true, then *The first man to set foot on the moon is American* is also true. Since *The first man to set foot on the moon has only one leg* is false, then *Neil Armstrong has only one leg* is also false.

All this seems unsurprisingly and intuitively correct. But unfortunately there are some types of sentence where it does not work. Sentences about someone's beliefs are good examples. Consider the sentence *Barnaby believes that the first man to set foot on the moon is American*. This sentence is true if it gives us an accurate account of Barnaby's belief. But if it is true, it does not necessarily follow that the sentence *Barnaby believes that Neil Armstrong is American* is also true. This second sentence may well be true but it does not have to be. To appreciate this we need only recognise that Barnaby may not have a clear idea of the name of the first man to set foot on the moon, or he may be under the mistaken belief that it was Buzz Aldrin. In either case we would have to conclude that the first sentence was true but the second one was false.

Sentences of this type are known as 'opaque contexts'; in a sense you cannot 'see through' from the truth of one sentence containing a particular reference to some extension to the truth of another that contains a different way of referring to the same extension. The opaque contexts concerned with states of mind such as beliefs are known as a statements of 'propositional attitude', because they describe an individual's attitude to a certain fact or proposition. Using a simple direct reference account of meaning, we would be at a loss to explain why opaque contexts do not behave exactly the same as any other type of sentence. If words simply identify extensions, then that is all they can do, regardless of the context.

Using Frege's distinction between sense and reference, however, we can explain what is different about opaque contexts. In cases where the actual means of identifying an individual is the most important issue, the sense rather than the reference of the relevant words becomes the most salient type of meaning. The sentences about Barnaby are about his attitude towards various possible statements, and therefore the exact words used are very significant. It is entirely possible that Barnaby might be prepared to agree with the statement *The first man to set foot on the moon is American*, but not with the statement *Neil Armstrong is American*. Since *Neil Armstrong* and *the first man to set foot on the moon* differ in terms of sense, sentences concerned with attitudes towards them can differ in terms of truth. Because it is the intensional rather than the extensional meaning that is significant in these cases, opaque contexts are sometimes also known nowadays as 'intensional contexts'.

3.4   Connotation and denotation

Frege's ideas have been extremely important to the ways in which people have thought about language, and particularly about how words work, but you will not necessarily find a lot of references to him in textbooks and general discussions of linguistics. It is not that linguists have forgotten about him, but rather that his solution to the problems posed by the direct reference account, and the more sophisticated thinking about meaning that he made possible, have developed a significance of their own beyond the work of an individual nineteenth-century mathematician. In a way this is quite a tribute to Frege; his original idea has become so central to present-day work on meaning that it has taken on a life of its own.

In linguistics nowadays the terms sense and reference are not much used. In discussions of these ideas you are much more likely to come across the terms connotation and denotation to describe very much the same distinction. 'Denotation' preserves the direct reference part; the denotation of a word, or what it denotes, is the actual thing or set of things that it identifies in the world. The word connotation needs to be treated with care because as well as its specialised use it is also used much more loosely in general everyday discussions of meaning. You may hear things such as 'that word has unpleasant connotations' or 'the connotation of what she said was that she was annoyed', where it is used to mean something like association and implication respectively. In formal discussions of meaning, however, 'connotation' has a much more specific use. Like the term sense, it refers to the way in which a word or phrase identifies an object: the particular manner in which it relates to its denotation.

Fully to explain the meaning of a word, then, it is necessary to describe both its denotation and its connotation. This has implications for word meaning that would be missed if we still had a simple direct reference account. Perhaps most significantly, it suggests that there are no exact synonyms in language. There are no two words in one language that mean exactly the same thing. Two words might well share the same denotation, or pick out the same set of things in the world, but they will always do so in slightly different ways from each other. They will have different connotations. For similar reasons, there are implications for translation. It is at least arguable that you can never achieve an exact translation between languages. It might be possible for one language to include a word with the same denotation as a word in a different language, although even this is far from uncontroversially true. But it might still be possible to argue that the two words differ in connotation, and therefore that they do not mean exactly the same as each other.

3.5   Use and mention

There is one more idea we need to consider while we are thinking about how words work. It concerns an aspect of meaning that is perhaps not so obviously in need of explanation, because it does not involve the type of everyday problems that we came up against when we started thinking about the direct reference account. Nevertheless there is a real issue to be explained about one particular way in which words can function. Like the distinction between denotation and connotation, this issue has been discussed for a long time in language theory, and has become part of linguistic description.

Think about this group of three sentences: *The President of the United States lives in the White House*; *The President of the United States is The Supreme Commander*; *The President of the United States is a definite noun phrase*. These three sentences all make sense and they are all true, yet they apparently say very different things about the same subject. With what we now know about sense and reference we can point out that the subject is not in fact exactly the same in the first two cases. In the first example the significant aspect of *The President of the United States* is its denotation; the sentence tells us something about the actual individual (whoever that is at the time) who is identified by this phrase. In the second example it is the connotation of the phrase that is significant. The sentence draws attention to two phrases with different connotations, and says of them that they will always share the same denotations.

But what are we to make of the third example? Neither the denotation nor the connotation seem to help us out here. It would be false and in fact extremely bizarre to say that a particular human being is a definite noun phrase, while the means by which we identify an individual is an idea or an aspect of understanding, not a piece of grammatical structure. Rather what seems to be at issue is the actual phrase itself: the particular set of words in the English language. In cases of this sort it has become customary to say that the phrase *The President of the United States* is not being used at all, as it is in the other two examples, but is simply being mentioned. Despite its apparent similarities with the other examples, the noun phrase in question does not actually occur in the normal way. It is simply being displayed, or shown, as an example sentence might be displayed in a linguistics textbook for the purposes of analysis and discussion.

Linguists have adopted the habit of using quotation marks to 'mark off' a word or phrase that is being mentioned. So while examples of use would be written 'The President of the United States lives in the White House' and 'The President of the United States is The Supreme Commander', an example of mentioning would be written '"The President of the United States" is a definite noun phrase'. The distinction between use and mention may seem rather esoteric, but it can be extremely useful when you are studying linguistics. You might, for instance, write 'Freddy is a nice chap' but '"Freddy" has six letters'; 'June is the sixth month of the year' but '"June" rhymes with "tune"'; 'Peter Pan is perpetually young' but '"Peter Pan" is alliterative'. However the distinction relies on the existence of words apart from their use, making them available to be mentioned. It is therefore compatible with the view that language is a state of mind, but is generally strongly rejected by those who argue that language can be explained only with reference to individual occurrences of verbal behaviour.

3.6   Further reading

See Jeffries (2006) Section 1.5.2 for more on sense and reference; Sections 1.5.4 and 6.5.2 for the implications in linguistics of connotation; and Chapter 6 for semantic links between words, including the possibilities of synonymy.

There are a number of detailed discussions of the origins of some of the ideas about words that we have touched on here. These include Chapman (2000, ch. 1), Stainton (1996, ch. 3) and Devitt and Sterelny (1987, part II).

The original account of sense and reference is Frege (1980, first published in 1892). This article is included in a number of anthologies and collections, but it is technical and quite heavy going. One thing to watch out for is that the original German title has been variously translated as 'On sense and reference', 'On sense and meaning', and 'On sense and nominatum'.

The distinction between use and mention has been discussed for a long time in the philosophy of language and linguistics. Its implications, particularly in relation to the use of quotation marks to show that a word is being mentioned, are discussed in the Introduction to Linsky (1952). An alternative view, which is highly critical of the distinction between use and mention, can be found in Harris (1996, pp. 100–4).

4 How does Language Relate to the World?

4.1 Introduction

We saw in Part I that approaches to describing and explaining language can differ from each other a great deal. One thing they all have in common, however, is their acknowledgment that language functions at least in part in relation to the world beyond the individual speaker. Whether you view language as an observable pattern of human behaviour, as a mental structure, or as a system for communicating with other people, it remains the case that there must be a link of some sort between language and what we might describe as 'the world' or 'reality'. This forces us to confront the question of how exactly language relates to the outside world. As with so many of the most important questions about language, it may at first appear to be rather uninspiring, even trivial. However, it has intrigued serious thinkers about language for centuries, and given rise to some interesting and complex ideas.

4.2 Correspondence

One fairly obvious answer to the question of how language relates to the world, which has an appealing ring of common sense about it, is that language is a tool we use to describe the world. Using the vocabulary and grammar of our language, we are able to put together sentences that describe the world around us. Our knowledge of the language allows us to understand what descriptions are put forward by sentences such as *Tigers are found in the wild only in Asia* and *Milk bottles grow on trees*. Furthermore our knowledge of the world allows us to distinguish between these sentences by saying that the first is true and the second is false. The first gives an accurate description of how things are in the world, while the second does not.

This common sense version of how language works relates pretty closely to what is known in philosophy as the correspondence account. Like many philosophical descriptions of language, the correspondence account is concerned primarily with truth: with describing meaning in terms of the capacity of sentences to be either true or false. It is a very old philosophical theory that can be traced back to the work of Aristotle in the fourth century BC and has turned up in various forms since then. Since the development of logical notation it has been possible to summarise the correspondence account in the statement 'p is true iff p', where p is a variable that takes the place of any description of the world. The odd-looking word 'iff' is short-hand for 'if and only if'.

'If and only if' differs from 'if' by making what follows a necessary condition. For example, if you say *I'll go to the party if Geoff goes*, you are making a commitment that if Geoff goes to the party you will go too. But Geoff's going to the party is not a necessary condition for your going; you might decide on the day to go, even if you know that Geoff will not be there. On the other hand, if you say *I'll go to the party if and only if Geoff goes*, Geoff's going is a necessary condition of your going. You are committing yourself to going to the party only in the event that Geoff is going too. You cannot later decide to go to the party anyway, or at least not without going back on what you said. In practice we do not use the expression 'if and only if' very often in normal language use, but the abbreviation 'iff' is very useful in logic.

On first sight the logical summary of correspondence may look distinctly unimpressive. It seems to be telling us that something is true if and only if it is the case. But to understand its full significance we need to think a little more about the nature of that something, the description of the world, represented by p. We need to understand p as standing in for a thought or an idea about the world. When we are describing such thoughts or ideas we generally introduce them using *that*. For example we might *think that tigers are found in the wild only in Asia*, or *believe that milk bottles grow on trees*. In language theory the content of thoughts, beliefs and so on are generally known as propositions. This is a notoriously tricky term to define, and it tends to be used in different ways by different theorists. It may be easiest to think of propositions as little pictures of aspects of the world. When we express propositions in language we tend to do so by means of simple declarative sentences, such as *Spiders have eight legs* and *Milk bottles grow on trees*. But it is important not to confuse the proposition with the sentence that expresses it. Propositions are not declarative sentences. They are the contents of thoughts, and we might choose to express these thoughts using declarative sentences.

If we look back at the logical account of correspondence we can now see that there is a bit more to it than at first appeared. The logical variable p

stands in for any proposition. In the logical formula, p appears first inside quotation marks. The logical formula is telling us about a form of expression of p, or a way of putting it into words. So 'p is true iff p' tells us that any form of expression of a proposition – that is, any declarative sentence – is true only in the case where the picture of reality contained in the proposition is accurate. So this logical formula tells us about the conditions for the truth of every single declarative sentence in a language. It tells us that *Tigers are found in the wild only in Asia* is true if and only if tigers are found in the wild only in Asia, that *Milk bottles grow on trees* is true if and only if milk bottles grow on trees, and so on. You may feel, and if you do many theorists would agree with you, that this does not tell us everything we need to know about meaning, or about how language relates to the world. But at least we have taken a step in the right direction, and come up with a theory of meaning that both mirrors an aspect of common sense understanding and raises some further interesting questions and puzzles.

4.3   Truth-conditional meaning

A we have seen, the correspondence account is a theory that tells us about the necessary conditions for the truthfulness of a sentence that expresses a particular proposition. This notion of 'conditions' has been extremely significant in studies of meaning and of how language relates to the world. Some theorists have suggested that propositions set out a series of conditions that have to be in place for any expression of that proposition to be true. Propositions specify 'truth conditions', and the meaning of any declarative sentence consists of a particular set of these conditions. On their own they do not generally tell us whether a sentence is true or false, but they are enough to point us in the right direction to find this out. Once we know what the truth conditions of a sentence are, we can look at how the world is in order to decide whether they are in place, and therefore whether the sentence offers a true description of reality.

In effect the above paragraph can be summed up by saying that there is a distinction between truth conditions and truth value. The truth conditions for any given sentence are the set of descriptions of how the world has to be if the sentence is to be true. Traditionally there is just one truth value for any sentence; it is a straight choice between true and false. The truth conditions tell us what we need to find out about the world in order to decide about the truth value. We need to keep the word 'traditionally' in mind because although in early accounts of meaning it seemed quite acceptable to say that there were just two truth values, true and false, later work in this area has raised problems with this. We will return to this issue in Chapter 8. Because of the distinction between truth conditions and truth values, the meaning of a sentence is sometimes described as consisting of both an 'intensional' and an 'extensional' component. We saw in the previous chapter that these terms are sometimes applied to the meanings of words. The extension of a word is the actual thing in the world that it names, while the intension is the means by which it names that thing. Similarly the extension of a sentence is basically its truth value: the property it takes on when it is compared with how things are in the outside world. The intension of a sentence is the picture of the world that it expresses. This picture of the world, or proposition, can be judged to be either true or false.

The account of meaning in terms of truth conditions and truth values has a long and significant history in thinking about language, and is still very much around today in philosophy and linguistic theory. However in more recent years some problems with and limitations of truth conditional accounts have been identified. These are not significant enough for this way of thinking about meaning to be abandoned altogether, but they have drawn attention to some aspects of meaning that cannot straightforwardly be explained in these terms, and have therefore forced theorists to think about additional types of description.

We have restricted our discussion so far to declarative sentences used to express propositions. Of course there are lots of other types of sentence that are used to do lots of other things. Some people argue that a great weakness of the account of meaning in terms of truth conditions is that it can really only account successfully for one type of sentence. We might be happy with the truth-conditional account of *Tigers are found in the wild only in Asia*, but there does not seem to be any equivalent explanation for non-declarative sentences such as *Shut the door*, *Would you like to come out for a drink this evening?*, or *What is the quickest way to the nearest hospital?*. In each case it does not seem appropriate to set about trying to find out whether the sentence is true or false.

Note also that not even all occurrences of declarative sentences, which would seem to be prime cases for a truth-conditional account, seem to be particularly well served by this type of explanation. There are some uses of declarative sentences where truth conditions and truth value do not give us the full picture. Suppose that someone brags *My team will definitely win the cup this year* and a sceptical friend replies *Yes, and milk bottles grow on trees*. Our truth conditional account of *Milk bottles grow on trees* will lead us to conclude that the friend has used a sentence that is false. But this hardly tells us all we need to know about what the friend has said. The bragger would have the distinct impression that he or she had received a put-down: that the friend did not share the optimism. This is undoubtedly conveyed by the sentence that the friend chose, but it is a type of meaning that cannot be explained simply in terms of truth conditions. We will return in Chapter 7 to the types of problem raised for truth conditional accounts of meaning.

4.4   Analytic and synthetic sentences

In the remainder of this chapter we will continue to concentrate on sentences where truth conditions and truth values do seem to have something to tell us: declarative sentences used literally. We have seen that these are far from being the only things that a theory of meaning needs to explain. Nevertheless they have been extremely important to thinking about language over the centuries, and they are certainly central to any discussion of how language relates to the world.

So far we have been assuming that the way to assign a truth value to a declarative sentence is to compare the latter with how things are in the world. As we have seen, this is in line with the correspondence account, which tells us that if the description of the world expressed by a sentence corresponds to how the world really is, then the sentence is true. This worked well enough for our example sentences: *Tigers are found in the wild only in Asia* and *Milk bottles grow on trees*. But there are some declarative sentences for which there is no need to look at the world before we can assign a truth value. Consider *Black sheep are sheep*. To work out whether this sentence is true or false we feel no need to go out into the fields to look at some black sheep and find out whether or not they are sheep. Instead we sense that we can be confident that this sentence is true just by looking at it. In particular we can see that what is said about the subjects of the sentence, that they are sheep, is actually part of the subject itself. There are therefore no circumstances in which this example could be false. In this it is different from our tiger example. We can imagine circumstances that would lead us to decide that *Tigers are found in the wild only in Asia* might not always be true after all; for instance we can imagine the discovery of a rare species of native African tiger. But we simply cannot imagine any circumstances that could lead us to doubt the truth of our sheep example, or at least not without a radical change in the meaning of language itself. We cannot imagine anyone presenting us with an example of a black sheep that is not a sheep.

Our sheep sentence is an example of what is known as an analytic sentence. Basically we need rely on nothing more than an analysis of the sentence to decide its truth value. The sentence does express a proposition; it contains a thought that can be related to the world outside the language. But there is no need to compare this proposition with reality to find out whether the sentence is true. Note that this is also the case with some sentences that do not contain the repetition of any single word between the subject and the predicate; that is, between the subject and what is said about the subject. *Bachelors are unmarried* is a classic example of an analytic sentence. Again there is no need to go out into the world to find out about the truth value of this sentence, for instance by conducting a survey of bachelors and asking them whether they are married. The very word *bachelor* contains the feature of being unmarried as part of its meaning. In order to conduct that unnecessary survey we would have to start by collecting a group of unmarried people; of course we would conclude that the sentence is true. So analytic sentences are generally defined as those in which the meaning of the predicate is contained within the meaning of the subject. The subject may say more than the predicate, and it may say it in different words, but the crucial point is that – assuming we already know the meaning of the subject – the predicate does not tell us anything new.

The examples we have considered in connection to truth conditions, the examples where we have to look at the world to decide on the question of truth value, are a particular type of declarative sentence, distinct from analytic sentences. They are known as synthetic sentences. Something that is synthetic is made by bringing together a number of separate parts. Unlike in the case of analytic sentences, there is no necessary connection between the meaning of *tigers* and the meaning of *are found in the wild only in Asia*.

The distinction between analytic and synthetic sentences is significant in many theories of meaning, and we will look at one such theory next. Like so many of the ideas we are considering, however, the distinction between these two types of sentence is controversial, and by no means all language theorists agree that it even exists. This is largely because the very idea of an analytic sentence relies on the belief that words have meaning independent of any use. It assumes that just by knowing the language you know enough about the meaning of words, to analyse an analytic sentence and see that it is true. As we saw in Part I, many language theorists believe that words have meanings attached to them independently of any individual example of use. Many others, particularly those who describe language primarily in terms of behaviour or communication, disagree completely with this and argue that it makes no sense to talk about meaning except in relation to individual instances of speech or writing.

Certainly discussions of the distinction between analytic and synthetic sentences belong more obviously to those with an interest in language as a self-contained phenomenon that can be studied in its own right than they do to those with an interest in language as a system of communication that exists only in specific instances of use. To appreciate this we need only consider just how unlikely it is that we will hear many analytic sentences uttered during our daily interactions. *Black sheep are sheep* and *Bachelors are unmarried* may be fascinating sentences to some language theorists, but they are not the sort of thing that people often say. Analytic sentences are true in all circumstances; that is, they are necessarily true. For precisely that reason they are generally completely uninformative. They fail to tell us anything new about the world. When you do hear analytic sentences being used they are generally fixed idioms. There are expressions in British English such as *War is war*, *Boys will be boys* and *Eggs are eggs*. We might describe these as analytic sentences, but we are unlikely to hear them being used literally. They are normally used to convey some meaning beyond their literal and uninformative content: meanings such as *You can't complain when awful things happen once a war has been declared*.

In contrast synthetic sentences are exactly the sort of sentence that can be used to give interesting information because they bring together two entities, or an entity and a property, that do not go together just by necessity. You hear far more synthetic than analytic sentences in everyday language. Synthetic sentences can put forward any imaginable description of how the world is. Some of these sentences will have the truth value 'true' and some will have the truth value 'false'. Some synthetic sentences, however, present a problem for the idea that you can use their truth conditions as a way of finding out about their truth value. This problem is the topic of the next section.

4.5   Focus on verification

So far we have been thinking about synthetic sentences as statements about the world that we can compare with how things really are. We have assumed that synthetic sentences are testable, as opposed to analytic sentences, which do not need to be tested. But not all synthetic sentences are as easily tested as the ones we have considered. For example *There is an invisible elephant in the park* and *Florence has a guardian angel* are undoubtedly synthetic sentences; there is certainly no necessary connection between *invisible elephant* and *park*, or between *Florence* and *guardian angel*. However there does not appear to be any obvious way in which we could test them to decide on their truth value. We may well want to label these examples as unlikely or highly improbable, but we are not in a position to say for certain that they are false. The elephant and angel are not available for inspection in the same way as the habitat of the tiger. If meaning is defined in terms of truth conditions and truth values, then, it is unclear how we can explain what these new examples actually mean.

This problem was tackled by a group of scientists and mathematicians working in Vienna in the 1920s and 1930s. This group became known as the Vienna Circle. As individuals they worked on a lot of different projects, but the ideas with which they are collectively associated are those of 'logical positivism'. The members of the Vienna Circle wanted to define the appropriate type of language in which to discuss scientific knowledge and findings. In order to do this they needed to be able to say why a sentence such as *Iron expands when it is heated because heat increases the speed of the molecules* was acceptable in scientific discourse, but a sentence such as *Iron expands when it is heated because the Genie of Metal wills it so* was not. Neither was necessarily true; both were possible hypotheses about how a physical fact could be explained. But the second did not belong in a scientific discussion, and would have been disruptive if someone had tried to introduce it into one.

The logical positivists of the Vienna Circle decided to divide all the possible sentences in a language into two sets: those that were meaningful and those that were meaningless. They were concerned only with declarative sentences because they were interested in the language used to make observation statements about how the world was. The everyday use of language to ask questions, issue invitations or make requests (which we will consider in Chapter 7) did not interest them. In the set of meaningful sentences they included all analytic sentences because these could be discussed in terms of definite truth value. (Of course analytic sentences are necessarily true, and therefore are not always interesting in everyday life, but they can be important in scientific discussion and logical reasoning.) Secondly, they included the statements of mathematics and logic as meaningful. Sentences in this very particular class were not necessarily true, and nor could they be tested in terms of anything outside the systems of mathematics or logic. Finally, they included all synthetic sentences that were testable in relation to reality or, in the terminology of the Vienna Circle, were verifiable.

To say that a sentence is verifiable means that there is some process of experiment or observation that can be undertaken to determine whether the sentence is true or false. That is, it is possible to use the sentence's truth conditions to work out its truth value, or to attempt to verify it. The logical positivist position was based on what became known as the principle of verification. This was expressed in different forms by different writers. One widely consulted version was that put forward by the philosopher A. J. Ayer. Ayer was not strictly a member of the Vienna Circle, but as a young man he travelled from Britain to Austria to meet the group, and was very impressed by their ideas. His explanation is a useful one for us because he introduced these ideas in a form that was accessible to an English-speaking audience; the Vienna Circle had published almost exclusively in German. Here is Ayer's version of the principle of verification:

We say that a sentence is factually significant to a given person if, and only if, he knows how to verify the proposition which it purports to express – that is, if he knows what observations would lead him, under certain conditions, to accept the proposition as being true, or reject it as being false (Ayer, 1971, p. 48).

The criterion of verifiability is met, then, if we can think of a way to prove conclusively that the sentence in question in either true or false; that is, if we can think of a way to determine its truth value. Ayer used the word 'purports' because he wanted to emphasise that it was only sentences that came up to the standard of verifiability that could actually succeed in expressing a proposition: something capable of having the value of true or false. The emphasis on verifying statements explains the link that we considered in Section 1.2 between logical positivism and the inductive scientific method. The matter is complicated and not all historians of science agree on it, but in general the Vienna Circle is associated with the inductive method, with its emphasis on positive knowledge based on empirical evidence. Popper was reacting against the Vienna Circle, or at least against his interpretation of their ideas, when he put forward his views on falsifiability.

For the logical positivists of the Vienna Circle, all sentences that were not analytic, did not belong to the systems of mathematics or logic and were not verifiable were simply meaningless. They had no place in serious philosophical or scientific discussion because they failed to express any proposition, and could never be assigned a truth value. This might not at first appear to have been a particularly radical suggestion. Our sentences about the invisible elephant, the guardian angel and the Genie of Metal are easily ruled out as meaningless, and we might want to say that this is no bad thing. But lots of other types of sentences that people use in everyday life, and use seriously, are also ruled out. Consider *You lost your temper on that occasion because of the repressed anger you feel towards your father*, *This is a piece of art of the highest merit* and *God exists*. All are potentially serious uses of language. All express ideas that people are likely to have strong opinions on and want to argue about. But all are strictly meaningless under the verification theory of meaning. Suddenly the ideas of logical positivism seem a lot more sensational than they at first appeared, and it is no surprise to learn that they caused a huge controversy when they were made public, and were even denounced by some people as anarchic and amoral. The logical positivists claimed that all the statements of religion, aesthetics and speculative psychology were strictly meaningless because it was impossible to propose processes to verify any of them.

It is very important to recognise that in saying this the logical positivists were not saying that the statements of religion and so on were false. They were not saying, for instance, that God did not exist. Indeed this negative statement was no more verifiable than its positive counterpart. So they were not saying that statements of religious belief were all false, but rather that they had to be dismissed from serious discussion on the ground that they were meaningless. In practice, of course, logical positivism was just about incompatible with religious faith.

When Ayer decided to make the views of the Vienna Circle more widely known, he made clear the implications of their ideas in terms of the types of sentence that were meaningless. The consequences were far-reaching. To be added to the list of meaningless sentences were all those concerned with ethics, with events that had taken place in the past, and with other people's state of mind, among many others. None of these could be verified with certainty. In effect, then, Ayer was explaining how – according to logical positivism – a huge proportion of the language that people used every day was strictly meaningless.

We can sometimes attribute some significance to such sentences, but only if we 'translate' them into terminology that is more logically rigorous. The following expression of moral disapproval, *You acted wrongly in stealing that money*, does contain a meaningful element that describes factually what took place: *You stole that money*. The rest of the sentence, the part concerned with moral disapproval, is no more than an outpouring of emotion, adding nothing to the proposition expressed. A sentence concerned with historical events, such as *The Battle of Hastings took place in 1066*, cannot strictly be verified, but it can be viewed as meaningful if it is translated into a statement about our expectation of what sorts of evidence (documentary, archaeological and so on) we would come across if we looked into the matter. Statements about other people's state of mind, such as *John is sad*, need to be translated into statements about other people's physical state. Strictly speaking all we have direct evidence of is that John is pulling a sad expression or is crying. Our opinion that John is sad is actually a conclusion drawn from these observations: reasonable perhaps, but not in itself verifiable.

Ayer's standpoint, which reflected that of the logical positivists in general, was that a lot of the ways in which people used language in everyday situations was imprecise and illogical. When it came to rigorous scientific or philosophical discussions, these types of use should be either ignored or translated into language that was more rigorous. Since then many thinkers who have taken an interest in language but whose primary focus is logic or science have suggested that any aspect of a natural language that cannot be explained entirely in terms of truth conditions and truth values is simply an 'imperfection' and is best ignored. We will consider the implications of this approach in Chapter 8.

4.6   Further reading

For a discussion of pragmatics see Clark (2006). Chapter 2 of that volume takes as its starting point the problem that truth-conditional semantics does not always tell us all we need to know about meaning.

The discussion of propositions, and of their significance in explaining the relationship between language and the world, has a long history in thinking about language. Particularly significant in this regard is Frege (1980), an article we considered in the previous chapter in relation to word meaning. Frege talks about meaning in terms of the contents of thought. He also discusses the distinction between the intensional and extensional aspects of the meaning of sentences.

The correspondence account of meaning is also a topic of long-standing debate. The logical version of it that we have considered in this chapter was proposed by the logician Alfred Tarski (1944) in a complex and technical but very influential paper. His ideas were subjected to criticism and developed further by the American philosopher Donald Davidson (1967, 1979). In his 1979 work Davidson draws attention to the fact that Tarski's account of meaning can explain only declarative sentences, and he attempts to extend it to explain interrogatives and imperatives. Tarski's and Davidson's theories are discussed in Martin (1987, ch. 22) and Evnine (1991, ch. 5).

The origin of discussions of the distinction between analytic and synthetic sentences is generally taken to be the work of the eighteenth-century philosopher Immanuel Kant. His best-known work (Kant, 1929) is a notoriously difficult piece of philosophical writing; Kant's main ideas about this topic are discussed much more accessibly in Ayer (1971). A particularly interesting debate on this distinction in relation to different ideas about meaning is that between the twentieth-century philosophers W. V. O. Quine on the one hand, and Paul Grice and Peter Strawson on the other. As we might predict from what we already know about Quine's views on language, Quine (1953) argues that the distinction does not work because it depends on a concept of meaning that is independent of use. Grice and Strawson (1956) respond to this by supporting the distinction and arguing that such a concept of meaning is necessary.

As already mentioned, Ayer (1971, first published in 1936) provides an accessible introduction to the ideas of logical positivism, including an account of verification and its implications for various types of sentence. Ayer revisited these ideas some four decades later (see Ayer, 1976). In this work he maintains his logical positivist approach, but he could be said to have softened his stance on the meaningfulness of various types of sentence in everyday language. Logical positivism, and verification in particular, are discussed in Devitt and Sterelny (1987, ch. 11) and Chapman (2000, ch. 3).

CHAPTER 5

Is Language Like a Code?

5.1 Introduction

There is something intriguing about the idea of a code. Codes and code-breaking turn up in many war and spy films, and there are also famous real-life examples, such as the Enigma machine, which was used by the British during the Second World War to decipher encoded German messages. The intrigue is at least in part associated with secrecy. Codes allow people to pass on information that is potentially sensitive or dangerous, confident that only those who are in the know will be able to understand it. Those who do not know the code are left baffled as to what information is being conveyed, unless of course they are able to work out the rules for themselves, or 'crack the code'.

Secrecy is not the only reason for having a code. Sometimes codes are used to convey information over distances or in difficult conditions. Many of the most famous examples far predate communication technology such as texting and e-mail. Think of Morse code, for instance, where series of long and short marks, sounds or flashes stand in for each letter of the alphabet. It is traditionally used in circumstances where someone needs to get his or her message across quickly, but the person receiving the message is too far away to talk to. Similar things could be said about many other systems of communication, such as semaphore. Even someone who waves a white flag at an enemy army could be described as using a code, albeit a very simple one; to anyone who knows this simple code the white flag conveys the message 'I surrender'.

5.2 Sign systems

It might seem tempting to describe language as a code. A language functions to convey information between people, but only those who know the rules of the language are able successfully to interpret the information. Listening to a foreign language can feel a bit like receiving messages in a code you do not know; you can hear the message but you cannot understand the information it conveys. Even the idea of 'cracking the code' turns up in the case of language. When a document or inscription in an unknown language is discovered by archaeologists, scholars study it in an attempt to work out the rules of a language that was once spoken and written but has now been forgotten. Certainly the notion that a language is a type of code, or ideas closely related to this, have been around in theories of language for centuries, even millennia. In Part I, when we were considering the idea that language is primarily a means of communication, we looked at the work of the seventeenth-century philosopher John Locke. Locke described how language enabled people to put their thoughts into words and communicate them to other people. Later in the same work Locke wrote:

> The comfort and advantage of society not being to be had without communication of thoughts, it was necessary that man should find out some external sensible signs whereby those invisible *ideas*, which his thoughts are made up of, might be made known to others (Locke, 1993, p. 227).

To understand this passage it is important to know that Locke explained people's understanding and knowledge of the world in terms of a series of ideas that were built up in their minds as a result of all their experiences. In the extract he described how society depended on people being able to explain their individual ideas to each other. If there were no system for doing this they would all be trapped with just their own understanding, with no way of being able to compare notes with other people or find out whether they understood things in the same way. Language allows us to do these things. As we might expect, Locke's commitment to the idea that language was communication had implications for what he said about language more generally.

Locke described language as being like a code, although he did not use this actual term. Our ideas are invisible, but the words we use to express them are 'sensible', or able to be perceived by our senses: hearing in the case of spoken words and sight in the case of written ones. So our words form a code for the entirely practical purpose of transmitting our ideas to other people. This model of language is intuitively appealing, and it has been very influential in thinking about language, although as we will see it is not without its problems. According to this model a thought in the mind of one person is encoded into words. The words are transmissible; they can be sent as sound waves through the air or as marks on a piece of paper. Another person acts as a receiver of this transmission. Provided the receiver speaks the same language, she or he is able to decode the words back into thought. Human beings are not capable of passing thoughts directly from one mind to another; they do not have the power of telepathy. But language provides a way in which a thought in the mind of one person can, through a process of coding and decoding, produce a similar thought in the mind of another person.

Locke did not talk directly about words, but about signs. The idea that the function of words within the code of language is to act as signs has been one of the most influential and pervasive in the study of language. Again it is an intuitively appealing one. Every day we are surrounded by signs functioning within more or less complex codes that convey information to us. Traffic lights fulfil their purpose by means of a very simple code in which different coloured lights and combinations of lights act as signs of different instructions to drivers. Brand names and trademarks work because a single word or even a single image acts as a sign to potential customers of the qualities associated with the companies in question. And in cartoons just a few pen strokes can act as a sign of a famous person or type of person. In the same way, to describe language as a system of signs is to claim that it works because words 'stand in for' different objects and qualities. The structuralist approach to language, which we will consider later in this chapter, depends on the claim that language is a system of signs of the same type as traffic lights, logos and cartoons. The only difference is that language is much more complex than these and other examples.

5.3   Peirce's theory of signs

A number of thinkers have offered explanations of what it means to say that language is a system of signs. Some of these have attempted to give accounts of how all sign systems work, with language forming just one part of that explanation. One particularly important account of this type is that by the nineteenth-century American philosopher C. S. Peirce. He was not primarily concerned with a theory of language, rather his goal was to devise a system complex enough to explain all the different types of sign people encountered in their interactions with the world and with each other. So he was certainly ambitious; he hoped to describe all the different ways in which people made sense of their experiences and represented these experiences to themselves in their thoughts and to each other in their communication.

Not surprisingly, the system of signs that Peirce gradually developed in the course of his writing was very complex and contained a number of divisions and subdivisions. But primarily he identified three different types of sign, distinguished by the means by which they represented something to an individual. First, there were representations 'whose relation to their object is a mere community of some quality, and these representations may be termed *likenesses*' (Peirce, 1992, p. 7). The phrase 'community of some quality' meant that the representation and the object had some property in common; normally, as the term 'likenesses' suggests, this was some physical resemblance to each other. A portrait acted as a sign of a person, for instance, because to some extent it resembled that person. Peirce later labelled this type of sign an 'icon'.

Second, the relationship between another type of representation and the thing it represented 'consists in a correspondence in fact, and these may be termed *indices* or *signs*' (ibid.). Note that at this stage in his work Peirce was restricting the term sign to this type of example. He later extended the term to cover all the types of representation. In the case of a sign of this second type, there was some factual connection, or some relation of cause and effect, between the sign and the thing it represented. Peirce's own example was of a weathercock. It represented the direction of the wind to anyone who looked at it, but the way in which it did this was not arbitrary or random. In fact the orientation of the weathercock was directly caused by the direction of the wind. In his later classifications, as here, Peirce labelled this type of sign an index (*index* is the singular form of *indices*). An index was something that pointed at something else. We could think of various other 'pointing' signs as being included in this class. A signpost represents to us the direction in which a particular location lies, and does so not randomly but because it physically points in the direction of that location. If you point someone out in a crowd or a group photograph, your gesture acts as a sign of that person to your audience because of its physical direction.

In the case of the third type of representation, the relationship to the object 'is an imputed character, which are the same as *general signs*, and these may be termed *symbols*' (ibid.). According to Peirce, this type of sign was quite different from the other two in that there was no natural or physical connection between the sign and the thing it represented. On the contrary, in the case of symbols of this type the link between the sign and the object was simply one that was imposed by convention. The 'imputed character' that Peirce mentioned was a property that was imposed on the sign by outside forces: by human intervention. Our earlier example of traffic lights is a case of signs working as symbols in this sense. In other contexts there is no necessary connection between the colour green, say, and the instruction 'Go', but in the context of traffic lights green is a sign meaning 'Go' by convention. Most significantly from our point of view, Peirce included words in the category of symbols. Words represented objects not because of any natural or physical connection but simply by an 'imputed' or imposed relationship. This idea became enormously significant in language theory. Peirce certainly was not the first thinker to describe language in these terms, but his attempt to describe language as a type of sign system was an early version of a very significant development in thinking about language.

5.4   Focus on Saussure

The thinker most closely associated with the idea that language is a system of signs is Ferdinand de Saussure. At a time when linguists were concerned mainly with studying the history of languages, Saussure was interested in developing a theory of language in general. While working at the University of Geneva he delivered a series of lectures on this topic between 1906 and 1911. After Saussure died in 1913, two of his former students decided that his ideas were so important that they should reach a wider audience. They pieced together the lectures from Saussure's original notes and from what they and their fellow students had jotted down or could remember, and published them under the title *Cours de Linguistique Générale* in 1915. This was later translated into English and published as *Course in General Linguistics*. This is how we know today what Saussure was thinking about language early in the twentieth century.

In 'The Course', as it is often called, Saussure (1960) argued that there was no necessary link between a word and the object, action or property it stood for. This may seem like a fairly obvious point to have made, and indeed one on which linguists are nowadays generally in agreement, but that was not always the case. Both before and during Saussure's time there were people who claimed that every word was linked to the thing it stood for by some sort of essential or natural tie. Saussure's claim was that, on the contrary, the link between word and object was arbitrary. To back this up he drew attention to the differences between languages. There could not be anything necessary about the relationship between the sounds of the English word *dog* and the animal we call a 'dog' in English, because in French the sounds of the word *chien* served equally well for the same purpose. Since the link between word and object was not necessary or natural, Saussure argued, it must be conventional. That is, words worked simply because a group of people, or what Saussure called a 'community of speakers', agreed on the conventions for using them. The members of a community of speakers did not, of course, have to enter into any formal agreement about these conventions; they were simply something they learnt to conform to during the process of learning a language. If the community of speakers did not share and stick to these conventions, language simply would not work.

Saussure claimed that when linguists studied a particular language, they were actually studying how the people who used that language, the community of speakers, thought about the world. This idea has some very interesting implications, which we will consider in more detail in the next chapter. The reason why Saussure suggested that there was such a strong link between language and thought was that he viewed both the word and the object as mental entities. That is, they both existed only in the minds, or the thoughts, of the speakers of a language. So he argued that a word did not stand for an actual thing in the world, such as a hairy creature lying by the door, or even the collection of all such creatures. Rather it stoods for a concept: the idea people had in their heads when thet thought of the word *dog*. Saussure called this concept the 'signified'. Similarly the signified related within the language not to an actual series of sounds but to a 'sound image'. This is something like the sound you hear in your head when you think of the word *dog*. Saussure labeled this the 'signifier'. Each individual signified was linked to a signifier to form a unit of language known technically as a sign. Because the sign was formed by the link between two elements of thought, the concept (signified) and the sound image (signifier), its existence was purely mental; it existed only in the minds of the community of speakers.

When people learnt a language therefore, they learnt to conform to the accepted conventions for using its words. They learnt a set of signs. This in turn meant learning not just what signifiers there were in a language, but also what particular signifieds they were linked to. Concepts existed only because they were signified in a language. Languages determined what concepts there were for the community of speakers of that language, and therefore what made up 'reality' for this community. The particular concepts involved might well vary from one language to another, and therefore from one community to another.

For Saussure, as we have seen, within any one sign there was an entirely arbitrary relationship between a signifier and a signified. Saussure described this as the 'arbitrary nature of the sign'. However he did not claim that language was arbitrary in every aspect. The relationship within a sign might be arbitrary, but there was another important set of relationships in a language, namely those between the different signs. These relationships were not arbitrary; in fact they were structured into a highly regulated system. Signs derived their value not from any fixed relationship they had to the outside world, but from their place within the system of language. So it would be wrong to pick out any individual sign and try to explain it in isolation. Rather a sign had to be defined in terms of how it fitted in with, and crucially how it was different from, the other signs in the same system. To return to our earlier example of the sign *dog*, you cannot really claim to understand this sign unless you are aware of its exact position in the part of the language system that contains signs such as *cat, mouse* and so on. You have to understand how *dog* relates to these other signs, including what makes it distinct, or enables us to tell it apart from them.

So the signs of a language belong to an overall structure in which there is a specific, unique place for each sign. Saussure labelled this system *la langue*. This French word is often translated simply as 'language', but it is important to bear in mind that Saussure used it to describe something very specific. *La langue* was the highly structured system of interrelated signs, including the conventions of how they were used. It was learnt by learners of a language and was shared knowledge in a community of speakers. Saussure was aware that language was not just a set of conventions or a system of knowledge. It was also an activity, something people did whenever they stopped for a chat. In other words, account had to be taken of all the actual uses of language in a speech community: the conversations, rows, interviews and jokes. Saussure labelled this collection of uses *la parole*, which is sometimes translated as 'speaking'.

The distinction Saussure made between *la langue* and *la parole* may well have a familiar ring to it. It is very similar to the distinction that Chomsky made some fifty years later between 'competence' and 'performance'. Chomsky acknowledged Saussure as one of his influences, and is sometimes described as working within the tradition of the structuralist linguistics that Saussure founded. However there are also some significant differences. Most importantly, competence consists of the knowledge of a set of generative rules, whereas Saussure's *langue* was a system of differences and relationships between signs. As we saw in Section 2.2, Chomsky insists that linguists should study competence and that performance is of marginal or no interest. For Saussure *la langue* and *la parole* had more equal weighting; linguists should study both the system and the everyday use of the system.

An analogy often used to illustrate Saussure's theory, originating in 'The Course', is that of chess. The different pieces, such as queen, bishop and knight, have different values; that is, they can be moved about the board in different ways. The relationship between a piece, a signifier, and its value, a signified, is entirely arbitrary. It is only because of the particular conventions of the game that a piece that looks a bit like a horse can move in one way while a piece that looks a little like a tower can move in another. What is essential is that the players are able to tell the pieces apart; however well you knew the rules, the game just would not work if the piece used as the white queen looked exactly the same as the pieces used as white pawns. The set of rules on the different values of individual pieces make up the game of chess, equivalent to *la langue*. Any individual game of chess, an actual event taking place between two players who know the rules, can be likened to an occurrence in *la parole*.

The comparison with chess also highlights some important consequences of Saussure's theory for language change. Because the value of the chess pieces depends on convention, it is impossible for any individual player to change them. You could not suddenly declare that from now on you will be using the white queen as the black king and *vica versa*. If you tried this you would quickly find that you would be unable to play chess with anyone else. In the same way language displays what Saussure called 'the immutability of the sign'; individual speakers are powerless to change the language. If you tried using words in a different way from the rest of your community of speakers no one would understand you.

However, precisely because signs are arbitrary they have a tendency to succumb to outside pressures and change over time. So signs also display 'mutability', but in relation to whole communities of speakers over long periods of time rather than to individuals. Going back to our chess analogy, imagine that a group of players have lost the black king from their set. It would be perfectly possible for them to use a candle or a sauce bottle instead, but it would be necessary for all the players to agree to conventions for the use of this new piece. Over time they might lose other pieces, and substitute pepper pots, marker pens and toy soldiers, until it could be said that the game itself had changed. In the case of language, of course, it is not possible literally to lose words as you can lose chess pieces. But as the needs of a community of speakers and what they have to talk about change over time, signs can change their value, or can come into or go out of a language. This is possible precisely because individual signs are arbitrary, conventional and therefore subject to change.

Saussure hoped that his theory of language could eventually take its place in a much broader study, or science, of human signs in general. He labelled this science 'semiology'. His idea was that all systems of signs, including language but including also systems such as architecture, fashion and law, would be fully understood once researchers were are able to identify and describe the structures that linked the different signs together. For this reason the school based on Saussure's way of thinking about language is known as structuralism.

5.5   Signs and intentions

The theory that language is like a code in which words act as signs of ideas in order to convey them from one person to another has a number of implications that have been questioned in linguistics. For instance, it has implications for the relationship between language and thought, and we will consider this in the next chapter. The claim that, although language may be one of the most complex systems of signs there is, it is no different in type and in how it works from any other system of signs, also has implications for the relationships between the different languages of the world. If there is nothing particular about languages that distinguish them from other sign systems, apart from their complexity, then there is no reason why the different languages of the world could not differ from each other without limit in terms of how they are structured. This implication is very much at odds with the idea that all human languages have certain universal properties in common: the view that follows from the idea we considered in Section 2.2 that language is a state of mind.

Questions have also been raised about what might be described as the mechanistic account of communication that the code model suggests. Theorists have wondered whether it really is possible for a thought to be put into words, and for those words to be translated directly back into the same thought. Intuitively there seems to be something missing from this account: something about the state of mind of the speaker who has decided to communicate in the first place, or the process of interpretation performed by the hearer. One thinker who tried to include these missing factors in an account of language was Paul Grice, who is now best known for his theory of conversational implicature.

In 1957, some time before he produced the lectures that set out the theory of conversational implicature, Grice published an article in which he made some suggestions about how language worked as a vehicle for communicating ideas between people. His main focus was the various different ways in which things could be said to have meaning. He was looking at language, certainly, but also at other phenomena that had different types of meaning. Like many others before him he was interested both in how language worked and in how it fitted in with and compared to other things that conveyed information.

Grice's article begins with a consideration of some of the ways in which various forms of the word *mean* are used. These uses describe ways in which we understand information about the world. One use is in cases such as Grice's example: *Those spots mean measles*. Here we might say that there is a link of cause and effect, or a natural connection between the piece of information (*The patient has measles*) and the vehicle by which this information is conveyed (*the spots*). Grice labelled this type of example a case of 'natural meaning'. A different type of case is illustrated by Grice's example *Those three rings on the bell (of the bus) mean that the bus is full*. Here there is no necessary or natural connection between the sound of the bell being rung three times and the piece of information *The bus is full*. Rather there is agreement between the relevant people, presumably the bus conductor and the driver, that the rings on the bell are associated with this piece of information. Grice described this as an example of 'non-natural meaning'.

Grice did not actually mention Peirce, but it is not hard to spot some similarities between his distinction between natural and non-natural meaning, and Peirce's distinction between different types of sign. Grice's 'natural meaning' looks a lot like Peirce's category of 'index'; there is a link between the piece of information and the sign that conveys it such that the information causes the sign. 'Non-natural meaning' is very like a symbol; the relationship between sign and information is arbitrary and imposed. Grice avoided using the terminology of signs. He preferred 'means' because it seemed to him to be more in line with how ordinary people, as opposed to theorists and philosophers, talked about the ways in which information was conveyed.

The crucial difference for Grice between natural and non-natural meaning was not just the type of link between information and sign, as it was for Peirce, but also the fact that in the latter case, but not in the former, there was someone intentionally 'doing the meaning'. When you say *Those spots mean measles* you are not implying that any individual actually means anything. A case of the measles just naturally causes the spots. But if you say *Those three rings on the bell (of the bus) mean that the bus is full* then you are implying that someone means something. The rings on the bell are not a natural consequence of the fact that the bus is full; they depend on a conscious decision on the part of the conductor to convey that piece of information to the driver by means of a pre-arranged code. To understand that there is no natural link you only have to realise that the conductor can ring the bell and convey the same meaning even if there is plenty of room on the bus. He might be under the mistaken belief that the bus is full, or he could be keen to finish his shift and is therefore hoping to deceive the driver into moving on. Either way he will still be ringing the bell in order to mean *The bus is full*. On the other hand, if there is no case of measles there is no way in which there can be spots that naturally mean the patient has measles. It might of course be possible for someone to have painted fake spots on the patient in an attempt to fool the doctor. But this would no longer be a case of natural meaning because someone would have (deceptively) meant something by the spots.

Not surprisingly, just as Peirce described language as a type of symbolic meaning, for Grice language was one example of non-natural meaning. We could say that the utterance *The bus is full* would operate in much the same way. It would convey by means of a shared code information that the conductor intended the driver to believe. Because of how he defined non-natural meaning, Grice had added a crucial new element to the account of communication. Communication no longer depended just on the existence of a shared code, but on something about the mental state of the speaker; what was most important was what the speaker intended to communicate. It was also crucial that the hearer recognised this intention; the mental state of the hearer became important as well.

The three rings and the utterance *The bus is full* are both examples of communication, and as such depend on the successful recognition by the hearer of the speaker's intention to communicate. The case where someone paints spots on the patient in the hope that the doctor will misdiagnose measles is not a true case of communication because there is no intention that an intention to communicate be recognised; in fact the prankster is hoping that the doctor will *not* recognise that there has been intentional human intervention.

The difference between the rings on the bell and the utterance *The bus is full* points to some of the reasons why the explanation 'language is like a code' has its limitations. Grice was aware of these limitations but he did not go very far towards addressing them in the article on meaning. The ringing of the bell is exactly like a code. It has been agreed in advance that three rings convey the information that the bus is full between two people who may be too far away from each other to speak or signal. Until and unless the rules of the code change, three rings on the bell will always convey the same piece of information. But the same set of words could convey completely different pieces of information on different occasions, without any change in the language. Consider the example *He is a fine friend*. We might consider that, between two people who speak English, this could be used to convey the information that a particular individual is a good and reliable ally. Note in passing that the pronoun *he* can refer to an unlimited number of male individuals on different occasions of use, so we can already say that meaning is not always fixed.

But worse problems are raised for the simple code theory of meaning when we start thinking about the different contexts in which the utterance might be used. Imagine that John has always declared himself to be a friend of Harry, but that Harry has just discovered that John sent a letter of complaint about him to his boss. Harry is discussing this with Martha and comments *He is a fine friend*. Unless Martha is very slow on the uptake she is unlikely to interpret this as meaning *John is a good and reliable ally*. She is more likely to interpret it as meaning something like *John is treacherous and hypocritical*. The rules of the language have not changed while Harry and Martha have been talking, so Martha must have been relying on something other than simply speaking the same language as Harry to have interpreted his meaning. Harry has not simply encoded his thoughts mechanically according to the rule of the language. And indeed Martha cannot be sure that the thoughts in Harry's head have simply been transferred into hers. She may not be aware of the exact nuances of what Harry is thinking, for instance of how John's previous protestations of loyalty are making Harry feel particularly bitter about this betrayal. However we can still say that Harry has communicated something to her by his words, and done so successfully.

Problems of this sort show up the limitations of a straightforward belief that language is like a code. We will consider some possible solutions to these problems, including that suggested by Grice himself, in Chapters 7 and 8.

5.6   Further reading

See Chapter 1 of Jeffries (2006) for structuralist ideas, and Section 7.3.2 for a discussion of the operation of Grice's 'cooperative principle' in conversation.

In Clark (2006, ch. 1) there is a discussion of language change and variation. Many see Saussure as having set the scene for work in these areas through his interest in language in speech communities and across time. Section 2.4.2 of Clark's book discusses Grice's later work on conversational implicature, in which he expanded his idea that the message being conveyed depends on being able successfully to recognise the speaker's intentions.

There are many introductions to structuralism in particular and to semiotics more generally, including Peirce's system of signs. These include Hawkes (1977) and Clarke (1987). The latter also includes a discussion of Grice's work on meaning. Later developments of structuralism and semiology include Barthes (1968) and Kristeva (1989).

Grice's account of meaning has been the subject of a number of books in its own right. These are generally philosophically quite dense and include Schiffer (1972) and Avramides (1989). It is also the subject of Chapter 4 in Chapman (2005). The idea that language works by the processes of encoding and decoding is discussed, and some of the problems with it are identified, in Sperber and Wilson (1995). Their ideas on this are discussed in Blakemore (1994).

How is Language Related to Thought?

6.1   Introduction

The nature of thought, and of the process of thinking, is a topic of enduring interest to human beings. Thinking is something that we do all the time; many people would claim that is is part of what makes us human. It is a hugely varied activity, including big intellectual endeavours as well as everyday decisions, speculations and daydreams. It is also notoriously difficult to explain. To do so involves a complex type of introspection; that is, it involves 'looking inside' ourselves and trying to figure out what we are doing as we think. This problem of introspection is particularly pressing when it comes to sorting out the relationship between thought and language. Just try thinking about the question 'Can I think without using language?'.

There are opposing answers to this question, both from popular opinion and from language theorists. Some people are convinced that they can think without using words, and therefore that thought and language must be two separate systems. This picture is apparent in the work of thinkers such as John Locke. As we saw in Chapter 5, Locke described thoughts as existing in people's minds and words as the vehicle by which they could be conveyed to others. Others have argued that you cannot think at all without using words, and that people who imagine that they think without language are just not good enough at distancing themselves from their own mental processes to be introspective about how those processes work. This is also reflected in the work of some of the other theorists we have considered. For instance Ferdinand de Saussure's claim that any individual language offered a unique set of 'signifieds', or mental concepts, suggests that you need to be in possession of a language before you can be fully in a position to think about the world.

Our language itself, or our everyday way of talking, does not offer much help in solving this problem. We talk about putting our thoughts into words, as though our thoughts existed independently and language were just a means of expressing them. However we also talk about thinking aloud, as though talking through a problem were just a more public version of what we would be doing anyway: using language to represent our thoughts to ourselves in our head. In this chapter we will look at some of the claims that have been made about the relationship between language and thought. We will start by considering in a little more detail the implications of Saussure's claim about mental concepts.

6.2 'Thinking in words'

As we have seen, Saussure viewed language as a system of relationships not between words and objects but between sound images and concepts. It was possible for languages to differ from each other not just in the words they contained, but also in the individual concepts those words stood for. One implication of this is that you need to learn the language of your particular society not just to be able to communicate with the people around you, but also to understand the world in the same way as they do, or to share the concepts with which they make sense of the world. For Saussure the relationship between the language people spoke and the way they thought about the world was a very strong one. He suggested that language and thought were linked as closely as two sides of a sheet of paper; the sides might be different from each other, but if you cut one side you could not avoid cutting the other side too.

This view of the relationship between language and thought implies that you need a language not just to appreciate how a particular society of people understands the world, but also in order to have any clear understanding of the world at all. Without language you would not have access to a set of concepts that make sense of the world, or to a system capable of joining those concepts together in different combinations. In other words, according to Saussure's structuralism a fully complex, structured language is a prerequisite for complex, structured thought. This idea has been pervasive in many subsequent works on language, and indeed it has a certain intuitive appeal. For the reasons we have just been considering, it is almost impossible to imagine what it would be like to think without the aid of the words we have learnt in order to label our experiences, and of the ways in which those words can be combined to give more complex descriptions of the actual or possible relationships between those experiences.

There are some striking consequences of this idea. If the possibility of thought really does depend on the possession of a language, and if language is a uniquely human capacity, then it must be the case that non-human animals are not capable of thought. The same must apply to people who do not have language because of their age or an incapacity. In the past, some writers have apparently been quite happy with this proposition, and have been dismissive of the mental capacity of, for instance, deaf mutes. People's inability to express themselves in spoken language has been taken as evidence of their inability to think beyond the level of basic physical and emotional responses. This in turn has had implications for the rights afforded to deaf people and the way in which they have been treated by society.

Nowadays few people if any would see the inability to speak as evidence of an inability to think. This change has been brought about at least in part by a better understanding of sign language. In recent decades a lot of work has gone into understanding and analysing the sign language – or more accurately the various sign languages – used by the deaf. Just as there are many different spoken languages used in different parts of he world, so too there are many different sign languages. It was once assumed that sign languages were basically sophisticated systems of gestures, elaborations of the types of paralinguistic gestures that accompany speech. More recently researchers have found that they are in fact a totally different type of system from gesture, and they are just as complex and expressive as any other human language.

Perhaps the most intensively studied is American sign language (ASL), but research has shown that observations about the general properties of ASL apply to the other sign languages too. ASL has been successfully analysed using all the usual forms of linguistic description. It has phonetics and phonology, in that signs are made up of individual constituents that can be combined in different ways to make meaningful units. It also has a complex grammar that determines how these meaningful units can be combined to form phrases and sentences. Grammatical rules that have been identified in ASL include those for negation, questions, plurals, pronouns and the agreement of verbs.

Research of this type has led to widespread acceptance that the definition of human language should to be broadened to include sign language as well as spoken language. It is therefore no longer valid to claim that if language is necessary for thought, deaf mutes must be incapable of thought. However it remains the case that the strong link between language and thought suggests that children are not capable of complex thought before they learn a language. The ability to think about the world around us beyond our own physical and emotional feelings must develop only once we master an understanding of language. This may seem like a perfectly reasonable position to take, but it does raise some interesting questions about how a process as complex as learning a language is possible in the first place.

6.3   The language of thought

The problem thrown up by the apparently close relationship between language and thought is something of a classic chicken and egg conundrum. It might seem reasonable to claim that we need a language before we can have thought, but then if we did not have thought how could we do something as intellectually challenging as learning a language? It almost seems that you need a language in order to think and therefore to be able to learn a language. In fact this is precisely what has been suggested as one answer to the problem. It has been proposed that, before the process of learning even a first language begins, human beings already have a language in which they think. It is a fully developed language, but not the same as any of the languages spoken in the world. By this means children are able to undergo the intellectual process of working out and learning the language spoken around them.

This idea has been around in one form or another for a long time. It has been traced back to the work of St Augustine, a Christian scholar who lived and worked in the fourth and fifth centuries AD. However the idea was revived and given perhaps its most extreme expression by the philosopher Jerry Fodor in the 1970s. Fodor's ambitious plan was to construct a theory that would explain how thought was possible (Fodor, 1976). He claimed that all thought processes could be described as 'computations'; every time people made a decision, figured out a problem or even just made a judgment about what they were experiencing they went through a series of processes rather like those performed by a computer. Any set of computations needed what Fodor called 'a representational system'. That is, there had to be a way of using symbols to stand in for the processes involved. For example, in order to do mathematics there was a system of numbers and ways of combining them; in order to perform its operations a computer used binary code. Fodor argued that we needed a similar system to represent the computations that made up our thought processes.

Fodor then set about establishing what this system must be like. He considered some of the relevant thought processes: reasoning and perceiving (making sense of the world) as well as learning, including learning a language. He concluded that the representational system must be very complex indeed, in fact it should be just as complex as any of the natural languages, such as English, French or Hindi. For this reason he described the representational system as the 'language of thought' (LOT). Fodor dismissed the possibility that the LOT for any individual might simply be his or her first language: in other words, when people thought they used the language they had learnt. He pointed out that there were creatures that did not have a natural language but nevertheless seem to think. Non-human animals went through processes of reasoning and decision making that enabled them to survive. And children thought before they learnt a language. This last point of course introduced the problem of language learning that we have already considered. Some of the most complex thought processes that children go through are those involved in learning a language. Yet Fodor thought that children needed a representational system as complex as a language before they could do this; in his words, 'One cannot learn a language unless one has a language' (ibid., p. 64).

Clearly the LOT could not itself be something that people learnt before they learnt English or French or Hindi, because to go through the process of learning the LOT they would need yet another representational system, presumably just as complex as a language. This further representational system would itself have had to be learnt, necessitating yet another representational system. This would lead to what is known as an infinite regress: the solution to one problem throws up a further problem, and so on without end. So Fodor proposed that, unlike natural languages, the LOT was not learnt. Rather it was an innate part of the mental structure of a creature. He was most interested in the LOT that was innate in human beings, and he examined the structure of natural language in order to consider in more detail what it must be like.

Fodor reached a conclusion that he admitted was rather hard to accept. The LOT must be not only as complex as a natural language, but also very similar to it in design and expressive power. It must have a similarly extensive vocabulary, and an equally complex syntax. Fodor argued that we could not learn the meaning of a word if we did not already have a mental representation equivalent to that meaning. We could not learn how to use the sentences of a language to express thoughts if we did not already have a system for representing to ourselves any thought that we could express in that language. He offered one consolation for accepting his theory about the LOT. It might be difficult to take on board the idea that we had an innate language, different from any of the natural languages that we might learn but remarkably similar to them. But if this were the case it would at least explain the apparent ease with which children learnt any of the natural languages. Perhaps natural languages were all dependent on the structure of the LOT, which was itself innate to human beings.

As he built up his case for the LOT, Fodor presented some interesting views on the role and importance of theory. He readily admitted that he was dealing with ideas that could not be proved, and for which he had no irrefutable evidence. He was exploring an area that was extremely important and interesting, but for which there was no direct evidence. When discussing the nature of human thought anything people said must necessarily be theoretical. As Fodor himself put it, 'remotely plausible theories are better than no theories at all' (ibid., p. 27). Although he did not express it in these terms, Fodor put forward a staunch support of the deductive method. Just because he was dealing in theory did not mean he was indulging in pure speculation without any grounding in reality. In fact he insisted that there was a solidly empirical basis to what he was doing. His theory about the complexity of the LOT was based on careful attention to the processes that it had to be able to explain, particularly to the nature of the natural languages that it enabled people to learn. Someone might well want to challenge his rather unpalatable LOT hypothesis, but the onus would then be on that person to come up with an alternative that still explained the observable facts about language. A theory did not have to be decisive, to solve all the problems and to be generally accepted in order to have something interesting to say. Fodor observed that 'saying the last word isn't the problem that currently confronts us. Our problem is to find something – almost anything – that we can say that's *true*' (ibid., p. 195).

Although Fodor's theory of an innate language that was just as complex as any natural language was extreme and controversial, many people have accepted a weaker version of it. They agree that some sort of representational system must be innate in human beings to get us started on the process of learning a first language. As we saw when we considered Chomskyan linguistics in Section 2.1, the so-called 'innatist hypothesis' has a different take on what must be innate. According to this hypothesis, human beings are born with a universal grammar that is compatible with all human languages. In Chapter 9 we shall consider the implications of this hypothesis for the question of how a child manages to learn a first language.

6.4   Focus on determinism

The theories we have considered in this chapter have in general been based on the premise that we need a language of some sort in order to think. In other words our thoughts are dependent on our language. As we have seen, this has some uncomfortable implications and, particularly latterly, linguists have been careful to define language as inclusively as possible in relation to this claim. However the dependence of thought on language in many ways remains unavoidable. This was acknowledged back in the 1920s by Edward Sapir, an American anthropologist and linguist. Sapir commented that:

> Many people, asked if they can think without speech, would probably answer, 'Yes, but it is not easy for me to do so. Still I know it can be done.' Language is but a garment! But what if language is not so much a

garment as a prepared road or groove? . . . The writer, for one, is strongly of the opinion that the feeling entertained by so many that they can think, or even reason, without language is an illusion. The illusion seems to be due to a number of factors. The simplest of these is the failure to distinguish between imagery and thought. As a matter of fact, no sooner do we try to put an image into conscious relation to another than we find ourselves slipping into a silent flow of words (Sapir, 1970, p. 15).

Sapir's contrasting metaphors of language as a garment and language as a prepared road are interesting. He was arguing against what he saw as the popular belief, held by most people, that language was something that was put on top of, or 'dressed up' pre-existing thoughts. Rather, he suggested, language directed thought as it progressed, rather like rails direct the progress of a tram or train. It might be possible to summon up images without words: to picture individual people and things. But this was not the same as saying we could have thought without language. As soon as we started to envisage possible relationships between individuals – in other words, as soon as we started thinking about things – we found ourselves using words in our head.

Sapir went a bit further than just commenting that he personally believed that we needed language in order to think. By doing so he contributed to the development of an idea that has become known as 'linguistic relativity' or 'linguistic determinism'. This has been an extremely important idea in terms of how people have thought about language. Not many people agree with Sapir wholeheartedly any more, but you will still come across references to his central idea. A clue to its development can be found in Sapir's metaphor of language being like a train track. A train track is not just there for the train to run on, it actually dictates, or determines, which way the train will go. The train is not free to move other than on the course laid down by the track. In a similar way, Sapir suggested, our thoughts may be determined by the language we speak.

This idea was developed in much more detail by Benjamin Lee Whorf, another American linguist and anthropologist who was Sapir's student, and who wrote about language in the 1930s and 1940s (Whorf, 1956). Whorf was particularly interested in the languages of Native American tribes. He travelled extensively around America and made notes on the languages he found, many of which were in decline or about to die out. Whorf was struck by what he saw as the vast differences between the languages he was studying, and between those languages and English. He was keen to point out that there was no difference in sophistication, or in expressive power, between a Native American language and English; he did not share the view of some of his contemporaries that the former were languages of 'savages' and as such were inferior and inadequate.

However, Whorf claimed to find striking differences in both the vocabulary and the grammatical systems of the languages he studied. Perhaps the most famous example of this was his observation about the different words for *snow* in the Eskimo (or Inuit) language. According to Whorf, Eskimo had three different words whereas English had just one, *snow*. These words could not be translated exactly into English, and to describe their meaning would require the use of more complex phrases, such as *falling snow, snow on the ground* and *snow packed hard like ice*. Whorf's original observation has since been much exaggerated and taken on a life of its own, and some people have claimed that there are 10, 20, or even 30 different words for snow in the Eskimo language.

Another of Whorf's claims, which is less well-known but just as striking, was that the language of the Hopi tribe had no words or grammatical constructions that related to time. As speakers of English we take it for granted that it must be possible to say things such as *I stayed five days*. Whorf claimed that it was not only impossible to say this in Hopi, but also that the language lacked anything resembling grammatical tense to distinguish between events that had taken place in the past and those taking place in the present. It is not that the Hopi made no distinctions between events, just that they divided events up differently. Their grammar allowed them to distinguish between events in terms of the validity attached by the speaker to the statement: roughly, whether the statement was a report of an event, an expectation of an event or a generalisation about events.

The significance of Whorf's writings on Native American languages has not been restricted to his ideas about the striking differences between different languages, interesting though these are. Whorf's work has been important in language theory because of the conclusions, or the wider claims, that he drew from these ideas. He argued that because speakers of Hopi had no linguistic means of expressing time, they were actually unable to think about time, and about the difference between past and present events, in the way that a speaker of English could. In a similar way, speakers of English could not fully understand the significance of the differences that were obvious to speakers of Eskimo; what to speakers of Eskimo were completely different entities and experiences were to speakers of English just different types of snow.

So it follows that the language you learn actually determines how you make sense of the world around you. It is not a case just of observing things and building up a picture of reality. Rather as you learn a language you learn certain ways of understanding the world, and it is not really possible to escape from or see beyond these. Your understanding of the world, and therefore the types of thought you have about it, will always be relative to or determined by your language. Here is Whorf's own account of this:

We dissect nature along lines laid down by our native languages. The categories and types that we isolate from the world of phenomena we do not find there because they stare every observer in the face; on the contrary, the world is presented in a kaleidoscopic flux of impressions which has to be organised by our minds – and this means largely by the linguistic systems in our minds. We cut nature up, organise it into concepts, and ascribe significances as we do, largely because we are parties to an agreement to organise it in this way – an agreement that holds throughout our speech community and is codified in the patterns of our language (Whorf, 1956, p. 213).

Here Whorf developed his own metaphor to describe the relationship between language and thought, based on the central idea of 'cutting'. As people interacted with the world they were presented not with a series of neatly separate phenomena, but with a potentially baffling bombardment of experiences and impressions. In order to make sense of the world they needed to be able to divide it up into manageable chunks, or to dissect it. They did not have complete freedom of choice about how to do this. On the contrary, the language they learnt specified how they would perform this process because the words available in their language, and the ways in which they could be combined, were based on a particular way of making sense of the world. It was this shared picture of the world, encapsulated in a shared language, that made communication possible.

The theory of linguistic relativity developed by Sapir and Whorf had an enormous influence on thinking about language. However over time some of Whorf's more extreme claims were discredited, or at least viewed with some scepticism. It was argued that Whorf had overestimated some of his findings. For instance when he stated that the Eskimo language had three words for snow while English had just one, he was ignoring related words such as *blizzard*, *avalanche*, *slush* and so on. More generally, linguists became uneasy with Whorf's claim that the language people spoke limited the possibilities they had for thought. Although few would now support Whorf's ideas in their entirety, many agree that a form of 'weak determinism' is useful or even necessary. Weak determinism is the name given to the idea that there is some causal relationship between the language we speak and the way we think about the world, that to some extent thought is determined by language, and that we should be aware that the picture of reality contained in any one language is not necessarily the correct or only picture.

6.5   Figurative thinking

One particular theory of language influenced by Sapir and Whorf's ideas about the relationship between language and thought is George Lakoff and Mark Johnson's work on metaphor. Lakoff and Johnson do not take a simplistic or straightforwardly deterministic approach; they do not claim that how we understand the world is a result of the particular language we speak. But they do take as their starting point the idea that 'a language can reflect the conceptual system of its speakers' (Lakoff and Johnson, 1980, p. xi) and they attribute this idea to Sapir and Whorf. A language has the potential to make available for inspection something that would otherwise be very hard to investigate: a particular mental system for making sense of the world. Lakoff and Johnson therefore propose to study a language, in this case English, in order to learn something about how speakers of that language understand the world.

The authors focus not on the vocabulary or the syntax of the language, but on the metaphors that commonly occur in it. Those language theorists who distinguish competence from performance would describe them as concentrating on an aspect of the use of language, rather than on the core features of the language itself. But Lakoff and Johnson reject this distinction, arguing that language in general and meaning in particular can only be explained with reference to how it is generally used in a particular culture. They also stress that in writing about metaphor they have not chosen a marginal or unusual type of language use. Far from being confined to literary texts, as some people assume, metaphor is pervasive in all types of language use even in the most everyday situations.

Lakoff and Johnson argue that metaphor is pervasive not just in language but also in thought and action. Human beings have a tendency to think metaphorically and to act in response to this way of thinking. The language we use also reflects this metaphorical way of thinking. To say that we think metaphorically is to claim that we often find it easiest to understand one area of experience in relation to or by comparing it with another area of experience. Lakoff and Johnson suggest that typically we understand abstract concepts such as emotions, relationship and ideas in terms of physical experiences relating to our bodies and the way they interact with the world. The abstract concepts are hard to think about directly, but thinking about them in terms of physical experience gives us a way of making sense of them. Metaphor is therefore a process by which 'human beings get a handle on the [abstract] concept – how they understand it and function in terms of it' (ibid., 1980, p. 116).

This way of understanding the world means that human beings accumulate a series of conceptual metaphors, in which one concept is related to another. Lakoff and Johnson give many examples of conceptual metaphors; one such is *Ideas are plants*. The existence of the conceptual metaphor gives rise to various linguistic metaphors in the normal use of language. So we have *That idea died on the vine, That's a budding theory, The seeds of his great ideas were planted in his youth, She has a fertile imagination,* and many more examples. In each of these linguistic metaphors ideas are talked about as though they were plants, and each draws on the general conceptual metaphor *Ideas are plants*. The collection of these linguistic metaphors in the language provides evidence of something that it would otherwise be hard to recognise: the existence of the conceptual metaphor as part of the system by which speakers of the language make sense of their experiences.

According to this view, metaphor is very far from being an added ornamentation in some types of language use. It is actually a reflection of how we think and therefore how we live our lives. The existence of all the individual linguistic metaphors shows that we do tend to think about ideas as though they were plants. There can be more than one conceptual metaphor attached to one area of experience. Something as important but as abstract as ideas is in fact a prime candidate to have several different conceptual metaphors attached to it. We have *Ideas are money (He's rich in ideas; He has a wealth of ideas; That book is a treasure trove of ideas)* and *Ideas are people (He is the father of modern biology; Whose brainchild was that?; Cognitive psychology is still in its infancy)* among several others. These different conceptual metaphors are the ways by which we make sense of different aspects of the concept.

Metaphors are so common in everyday language and some individual ones are so familiar that it can be difficult to spot that they are in fact metaphors and not literal descriptions. In other words we are not always aware of the conceptual system underlying the manner in which we make sense of the world, and therefore are not always open to the possibility that different systems might be equally possible. What is true for us is to a large extent dependent on our conceptual system, which is metaphorical. We make particular links between experiences, but there are other possible links that could be made. It follows that there is no such thing as absolute truth; what is true for an individual is a result of one particular metaphorical system. It is of course extremely difficult for us to distance ourselves from our conceptual system in order to become aware of it and to inspect its limitations. But Lakoff and Johnson argue that it is important to do this. They end their study with the conceptual metaphor *Labour is a resource*. People talk about *The cost of labour* and *The supply of labour*. They argue that the fact that labour is seen as commodity, like raw materials, leads to the unquestioning assumption that cheap labour, like any other cheap resource, is a good thing.

The exploitation of human beings through this metaphor is most obvious in countries that boast of 'a virtually inexhaustible supply of cheap labor' – a neutral-sounding economic statement that hides the reality of human degradation (ibid., p. 237).

So Lakoff and Johnson reach a conclusion about the significance of metaphor that is very definitely grounded in real world considerations. Metaphors are so pervasive that the conceptual systems underlying them can go unrecognised and the behaviour that results from them unchallenged. It can be difficult to recognise that a conceptual metaphor such as *Labour is a resource* exists, let alone that it is just one possible conceptual metaphor, and that there are other possible ways of understanding that same area of experience.

6.6   Further reading

See Jeffries (2006, ch. 1) and Clark (2006, ch. 4) for discussions of critical discourse analysis (CDA). Ideas about linguistic determinism have formed the basis of work on the relationships between language and ideology that is represented particularly strongly in CDA.

Saussure's ideas about the relationship between language and thought, like his ideas about language discussed in the previous chapter, can be found in Saussure (1960). Fodor's theory on the language of thought is presented in Fodor (1976), which also includes a discussion of some earlier thinkers who put forward similar ideas, such as Augustine. The topic of linguistic determinism is developed in Sapir (1970) and Whorf (1956), and it is discussed further, including its implications and limitations, in Devitt and Sterelny (1987, ch. 10) and Pinker (1995, ch. 3). Conceptual and linguistic metaphors and their implications for our world view are discussed in Lakoff and Johnson (1980).

How does Context Affect Meaning?

7.1 Introduction

As speakers of a language we have a sense that the context in which our words are produced can affect their meaning. Politicians are fond of complaining that their words have been 'taken out of context'. This suggests that to quote what someone said without giving sufficient information about the situation in which they said it is somehow to misrepresent them. If you ask someone what a word means, it would not be too surprising to be asked 'what's the context?', suggesting that it is easier to define a word in relation to a particular context than in isolation. These everyday attitudes raise some important questions. How can the context in which we speak be so significant that it actually affects what our words mean? What are the consequences of this for our attempts to understand and explain meaning?

As we have seen, strictly truth-conditional accounts of meaning cannot explain many of the ways in which meaning interacts with context. They cannot tell us what is going on when a sentence is used metaphorically or sarcastically. And they cannot explain the ways in which we use language not to describe the world but to issue orders, ask questions and so on. The most hard-line response to these issues from advocates of truth conditions is simply to dismiss them as imprecisions of natural language; a truly scientific language for describing the world would not contain such imperfections, but unfortunately individual natural languages are not like that.

In present-day linguistics, however, there is understandably more interest in explaining meaning in natural language. Linguists who want to include truth conditions as part of their account tend to argue that truth conditions can tell us something, but not everything, about meaning. These linguists generally make a distinction between semantics, which concerns literal meaning as determined by the language, and pragmatics, which concerns other types of meaning determined by context. The semantics of a sentence will contribute to what an utterance of that sentence means in context, but will not tell us the whole story because pragmatic factors will also have a part to play. The distinction between semantics and pragmatics only makes sense to those linguists who view language as existing independently of use. Semantics, after all, is part of the independent language system. So this approach to meaning is compatible with, although it is by no means restricted to, transformational grammar, in which linguistic meaning is determined by the rules of the language at the level of deep structure.

We will consider the idea that truth conditions tell us something but not everything about meaning in natural language in more detail in the next chapter. Some thinkers, however, have used examples of the shortcomings of truth-conditional semantics to argue that truth conditions are just not the right way to go about explaining meaning in natural language.

7.2 'Meaning is use'

As we saw in Part I, linguists who define language in terms of communication argue that to describe language it is necessary to describe how people use it in actual, individual contexts. For these linguists, the relationship between context and meaning is of paramount importance. Many would argue that it does not even make sense to try to discuss 'meaning' as a feature independent of context. The meaning of a word is entirely defined by how speakers use it in context; to suggest that meaning has some unseen, independent existence is to allow unjustifiable mentalist elements to creep into an account of language. In other words these linguists reject the distinction between semantics and pragmatics as an unnecessary imposition on human communication.

The basis for this view of meaning can be found in various philosophical approaches, particularly some that were developed in the middle part of the twentieth century. In many cases the philosophers who developed the view that meaning should be explained in terms of use were reacting against extreme 'truth' theories of meaning. For them the problems that theories such as verificationism ran into were just too big. They wanted to find an entirely different way of explaining how language works. This decision was necessarily based on a belief that natural language, far from being too messy and imprecise to be of any use to philosophers, was a valid focus of study in its own right and needed its own type of description and explanation.

A name that you will probably come across when you are reading about accounts of meaning based on use is that of Ludwig Wittgenstein. Wittgenstein was an Austrian philosopher who spent much of his working life at Cambridge University during the early and middle part of the twentieth century. He is credited with coining the phrase 'Meaning is use', and therefore with inspiring this whole approach to language. If you read his early work, however, you would not be able to predict that this would happen. In fact at the start of his career his approach to meaning was very definitely in terms of truth, correspondence and logic. But later in life he became aware of some of the problems with this, and he suggested instead that the meaning of words could be understood only in relation to how they were used in everyday interactions. Here is one of Wittgenstein's typically obscure sentences, in which he discusses the meaning of signs, or of individual words and sentences: 'The mistake we are liable to make could be expressed thus: We are looking for the use of the sign, but we look for it as though it were an object *co-existing* with the sign' (Wiggenstein in Kenny, 1994, p. 61). Here Wittgenstein is arguing that it is a mistake to think about meaning as something that exists alongside and independent of the particular word or sentence. So he not only defined meaning in terms of use, he also saw it as having no independent existence apart from individual instances of use.

Witgenstein was not the only philosopher prompted by the problems with truth-conditional accounts of language to look for another way of explaining meaning. At much the same time as he was developing these ideas in Cambridge, a group of philosophers in Oxford were thinking along similar lines. We will consider some of their ideas here because they are part of the reaction within philosophy against truth-conditional accounts of meaning. However, as we will see, they did not necessarily conclude that it was possible or desirable to equate meaning with use. This group became known as the 'ordinary language philosophers'. As this title suggests, they were convinced that ordinary language, the language that people used in their everyday interactions, deserved serious study in its own right. Any account of meaning would have to explain how it worked in ordinary language, not just in the technical languages of philosophy and logic. One of the most influential philosophers of this group, and the one who had the most to say about the importance of paying attention to the everyday use of language, was J. L. Austin. In many of his writings he attacked other philosophers for their reliance on specialised philosophical terminology, and for ignoring 'our common stock of words', or the resources available in ordinary language for describing experience:

> Our common stock of words embodies all the distinctions men have found worth drawing, and the connections they have found worth making, in the lifetimes of many generations: these surely are likely to be more numerous, more sound, since they have stood up to the long test of the survival of the fittest, and more subtle, at least in ordinary and

reasonably practical matters, than any that you or I are likely to think up in our arm-chairs of an afternoon – the most favoured alternative method (Austin, 1956, p. 130).

Here Austin was going further in his defence of ordinary language than just saying that it was worthy of study in its own right. He was actually arguing that philosophers would do well to use it as a tool in their studies. Ordinary language had developed and, in Austin's opinion, improved over generations of use so that it was now an excellent resource for discussing all areas of human experience. Careful attention to the meaning of ordinary language, which meant careful attention to the ways in which it was used, would give philosophers access to the ways in which human beings understood the world. Philosophers who ignored the resources of ordinary language and tried to think things through in isolation ('in their arm-chairs') were missing out on a lot of human common sense.

Austin put his ideas into practice and looked into the use of various areas of vocabulary. This involved a process that he described as 'linguistic botanising'. Comparing the study of language to that of an empirical science, such as the study of plant life, he argued that it was possible to collect examples of words and their usages and draw up a general picture of how the language explained a certain area of experience. Sometimes in collaboration with some of his Oxford colleagues, Austin would compile lists of related words, drawing on his own knowledge of the language as well as on dictionaries and other books. Then he would think about the possible contexts in which these words could appear, and the different meanings they would have in those contexts. This part was done through intuition, relying on his and other's own knowledge as speakers of the language. Austin argued that this process showed up the many inaccurate and counterintuitive ways in which philosophers tended to use language: ways that immediately cast doubt on the validity of their theories. He also discovered some particular ways in which people frequently used language that just could not be explained in a traditional truth-conditional account of meaning.

7.3   Focus on speech acts

In the course of his detailed and meticulous investigations of the words of the English language and how they were used, Austin noticed what seemed to him to be a special category of verbs. These could be used in such a way that they did not describe an action, as might be expected from a verb. Rather they actually performed an action. Think about the difference between *I add the beaten eggs to the flour mixture* and *I name this ship The Titanic*. Both are apparently straightforward declarative sentences with first person singular subjects and present-tense verbs. Both might be expected to offer a description that could be compared with reality in order to determine a truth value. This seems to work well enough for the first example. We can imagine the sentence being used during a cookery programme as the presenter describes what he or she is doing. It will be true if the presenter is adding the eggs to the flour. The second case, however, does not seem to offer a description of the action in question. The action is not taking place separately from the use of the sentence. The use of the sentence actually is the action. Once the sentence has been used something has been achieved: a ship has been named.

Because these verbs performed rather than described an action, Austin initially labelled them, and the sentences that contained them, 'performatives'. During the course of his own work on this topic, he identified a number of problems with the idea that there was a separate, identifiable class of performative verbs, and decided that this particular idea was not really workable. Nevertheless his work on performatives was the start of what has become known as the 'theory of speech acts', an approach to explaining meaning in context developed by Austin and others after him. It is still worthwhile to look at what Austin said about performatives because much of it remains relevant to the general description of speech acts. In the following passage Austin discusses some of the key features of performative utterances:

> In these examples it seems clear that to utter the sentence (in, of course, the appropriate circumstances) is not to *describe* my doing of what I should be said in so uttering to be doing or to state that I am doing it: it is to do it. None of the utterances cited is either true or false: I assert this as obvious and do not argue it. It needs argument no more than that 'damn' is not true or false: it may be that the utterance 'serves to inform you' – but that is quite different. To name the ship *is* to say (in the appropriate circumstances) the words 'I name, etc.'. When I say, before the registrar or altar etc., 'I do', I am not reporting on a marriage: I am indulging in it (Austin, 1962, p. 6).

Significantly, then, asking whether a performative is true or false is not an appropriate question to ask. If Austin was right about this, we are confronted with a whole set of cases where the account of meaning in terms of truth conditions and truth values cannot tell us very much. And intuitively this does seem to be the case. We can imagine contexts in which there would be something not quite right about uttering a performative such as *I name this ship The Titanic*. If someone who was not an invited dignitary and was not taking part in an official launching ceremony were to smash a bottle of champagne against a new ship and say this we might well want to object. But we would probably not say that what the person had said was false; rather that it was out of place, or just inappropriate.

Austin concluded that in the case of performatives the traditional concern with truth and falsity should be replaced by a discussion of appropriateness and inappropriateness. Just as there were truth conditions for descriptive utterances that helped to determine truth value, so there were particular conditions for performatives that established whether what had been said was appropriate or inappropriate. Austin described these conditions as 'felicity conditions'. Felicity conditions, as the name suggests, are concerned with specifying what makes a performative felicitous, or appropriate. They are the conditions under which a performative is appropriately used, and is therefore successful. In the case of the ship-naming example, for instance, the felicity conditions are all the factors that need to be in place for an official launching ceremony, an invited dignitary and so on.

Austin gave up on the idea of performatives as a separate class for a number of reasons. Not least he realised that acts could be performed in many ways that did not involve first-person performative verbs. For instance if you want to request that someone pass you the salt you could use an explicit performative and say *I request that you pass me the salt*, but you are much more likely to say something like *Please pass the salt, Can you pass the salt?* or *I could use some salt over here*. These alternatives all share a set of felicity conditions, and if these conditions are met they all succeed in acting as a request to pass the salt, but none of them have the formal grammatical properties that Austin originally identified for performatives.

So Austin kept the idea of felicity conditions, but concluded that they did not apply just to performatives. Instead he decided that when something was done using words there were three different things going on, or three different acts taking place. There was a 'locutionary' act, which in effect was the event of a particular set of words having been used. Then there was the 'illocutionary' act, which was what the speaker intended to do by producing this particular set of words in that context. Finally there was the 'perlocutionary' act, which was the result or consequence of the set of words having been used; often the perlocutionary act was concerned with some state of mind or response on the part of the person being addressed. For instance, in the case of the example *I could use some salt over here*, we could report on the locutionary act simply by saying that those words were uttered. To report the illocutionary act we would have to think about what the speaker was hoping to achieve; we might say something like *The speaker requested that the hearer pass the salt*. The perlocutionary act might well fulfil the speaker's hopes, but it need not. We might be able to report it by saying *The speaker persuaded the hearer to pass the salt*, but we might have to say *The speaker offended the hearer horribly*.

Speech act theory was subsequently applied to numerous types of discussion of language and was extended beyond Austin's original insights. Perhaps the most influential extensions were those made by John Searle (1969, 1979). In particular Searle used Austin's distinction between the different types of act, and particularly his identification of the illocutionary act, to define what he described as 'indirect speech acts'. Searle's discussion of these was concerned with one way in which the literal meaning of words could be different from the meanings they took on in particular contexts. The following passage discusses this difference, which Searle described as a difference between 'sentence meaning' and 'utterance meaning':

> One important class of such cases is that in which the speaker utters a sentence, means what he says, but also means something more. For example, a speaker may utter the sentence "I want you to do it" by way of requesting the hearer to do something. The utterance is incidentally meant as a statement, but is also meant primarily as a request, a request made by way of making a statement. In such cases a statement that contains the illocutionary force indicators of one kind of illocutionary act can be uttered to perform, *in addition*, another type of illocutionary act (Searle, 1979, p. 30).

Here *I want you to do it* is an indirect speech act. Its literal meaning makes it a statement, but this is not what is chiefly intended, so it would not give us an accurate description of the illocutionary act performed. Rather the primary illocutionary act, or the primary illocutionary force of the utterance, is that of a request. The literal (statement) meaning is not completely irrelevant. A statement is still made but it is not the most important thing done; it is the secondary illocutionary act.

Indirect speech acts are very common in everyday language. This is perhaps in part because they are generally considered to be more polite than their more direct equivalents. They are so common that many examples – such as *Can you pass the salt please?* – are almost always used with their primary illocutionary force rather than their literal meaning. Nevertheless felicity conditions remain the key to establishing what is intended. In many situations in which this sentence is used the felicity conditions necessary for a question (primarily, the speaker does not already know the answer) will not be in place. It would normally be extremely odd for a speaker to be inquiring about the hearer's ability to pass the salt. The felicity conditions for a request, however, are much more likely to be in place. These include the conditions that the speaker wants the hearer to do something, that the hearer is physically capable of doing it, and so on. Therefore the example is interpreted as primarily a request rather than a question.

Speech act theory, then, offers one answer, or one part of an answer, to the question of how context affects meaning. Clues from the context tell us what types of utterance would be felicitous, or appropriate. This in turn indicates how an utterance was intended: for instance as a request, a question or a statement. The intended meaning may be quite different from the literal meaning of the words used. Austin, Searle and others who have since worked with speech act theory are therefore committed to the idea that the meaning conveyed by an expression depends on how it is used. But note that they are not committed to the idea that meaning is just use. On the contrary, speech act theory relies on the assumption that there is something called literal meaning, which is attached to the words we use before any consideration of context. Otherwise it would not be possible to speak as Searle did of how intended meaning may differ from literal meaning, or how our knowledge of literal meaning and context together help us establish what speech act has been performed. For speech act theorists, then, literal meaning interacts with contextual factors of usage to give a precise picture of what was meant on a particular occasion.

7.4 Deixis

Non-literal meaning such as figurative uses of language, and the variety of different speech acts that people are able to perform with their words, are some of the most striking ways in which context affects meaning. But these are by no means the only cases where we may need to look at the circumstances in which words are uttered before we can obtain a full picture of what they mean. Indeed one characteristic shared by all human languages is that they contain words that rely on context for a large part of their meaning. Think about words such as *I* and *you*. As speakers of English we know what these words mean. This includes knowing that their meaning varies according to context. *I* refers to a speaker or writer and *you* to a hearer or reader, whoever these people may be on any particular occasion of use. Using the terminology we considered in Chapter 3, we could say that these words have a sense, or intension, but are dependent on context for the other essential part of their meaning: their reference, or extension.

Words such as *I* and *you* are described as 'deictic expressions', or as examples of 'deixis'. They derive their meaning from the way in which they point to some aspect of context. There are many different types of deictic expression besides personal pronouns. For instance there is a whole set that refer to place. The demonstrative pronouns *here* and *there* are good examples. Out of context, we know only that they have the potential to be used to refer to the location of the speaker and to some other location. The nature of these locations, and of factors such as how far *there* is away from the speaker, will vary from one context to the next. Some verbs contain deixis of place as part of their meaning. *Come* and *go* are both verbs concerned with motion, but the direction of that motion depends on the location of speaker and hearer.

There are also deictic expressions that are linked to context in terms of time of utterance. Many of the expressions that we use to indicate our relationship to past or future events vary in meaning from one occasion of use to the next. These include, for instance, *today, tomorrow, last year, next Tuesday* and *in three days' time.* Perhaps even more strikingly, the whole grammatical system of verb tenses is deictic. The general difference in meaning between *I am running, I ran* and *I will run* is determined by grammatical tense, but the actual difference of the timing of each event depends on when each is uttered. There is not a straightforward relationship between tense and time. When looking at the tense of a verb we do not automatically know whether the event described is positioned at the time of speaking before the time of speaking, or after the time of speaking. If we say *The plane leaves this afternoon* we use the present tense but refer to a future event. If we say *I wanted to speak to you in private* we use the past tense to refer to a present wish. But because the tenses link events to times, even if they do so in a complicated way, the system of grammatical tenses is described as deictic.

The deictic nature of tense is significant because it gives a clear indication of just how pervasive deixis is. Every major sentence in English includes a tensed verb. In fact the many different ways in which words point to an aspect of context mean that almost every time we say anything we are using at least one deictic expression. As well as the examples we have considered so far, there is the rôle that deixis often plays in determining the reference of noun phrases, for instance the difference between *This boy* and *That boy* and between *The man I met on the train yesterday* and *The man I met on the train today.* The fact that deixis occurs at all means that its effects on meaning have to be taken in to account, but the fact that it plays such a significant part in language means that it has potentially serious consequences for any theory of meaning. It is clearly not straightforwardly the case that linguistic meaning exists independently of context and is then simply 'filled out' on particular occasions of use by reference to figurative meanings, speech acts and so on.

Deixis presents a big problem for any hope of a straightforward distinction between semantics, which determines meaning out of context, and pragmatics, which augments that meaning in context. It challenges what is sometimes known as prepragmatic semantics, the idea that semantics provides a complete meaning that pragmatics can then work on independently. It seems that in many cases we need to know something about context before we can be certain what meaning pragmatics has to work on. *She will take it there tomorrow* does not tell us very much until we know more about the deictic meanings of *she, it, there* and *tomorrow*. We need to know these things before we can establish, for instance, what implicatures the speaker is conveying, or whether the utterance is intended as a promise or a threat. Worse still, the very principles that are generally agreed to be pragmatic might play a role in determining these aspects of meaning. For instance we might need to call on the idea of what individual is most relevant in the context in order to work out who *she* is.

In response to these problems, theorists working in the area of pragmatics tend to come to one of two conclusions. The first is to conclude that a clear-cut distinction between semantics and pragmatics is not possible. Semantic and pragmatics are not autonomous; that is, they do not operate independently of each other. In particular, pragmatic principles must play a part even at the point of establishing what proposition has been expressed on a particular occasion. The alternative approach is to insist that semantics is a separate system and does produce a complete proposition for pragmatics to work on. However propositions can be minimal in content; that is, they may consist of little more than an outline of the meanings that a sentence can be used to express in context. Very roughly the proposition expressed by the example above might be *Some female individual will take some object to a location that is to some extent distant on the day after this utterance*. Theorists who hold to each of these two positions have different views about the exact division of labour between semantics and pragmatics in determining meaning. Some of the work produced on either side is discussed in the 'Further reading' section at the end of this chapter.

7.5   Ambiguity

Language is often ambiguous. The fact that it still works successfully in communication, and indeed that in everyday use people are perhaps hardly aware of ambiguity, is because it is generally tied to particular contexts. Ambiguity occurs whenever there is more than one possible meaning for a word or expression. Sometimes it is important to a speaker that the hearer is aware of the ambiguity, for instance in the telling of certain types of joke. On many occasions, however, ambiguity is not an issue at all and may even go unnoticed, because in the context only one of the possible meanings could actually be intended.

Ambiguity comes in different forms. One very common type, known as lexical ambiguity, is where what appears to be a single word has two or more different meanings. In English *bank* can mean either the side of a river or a financial institution; *port* has many meanings, including a harbour and a fortified wine; *pen* can mean either an enclosure for animals, a writing instrument or a female swan. In these cases linguists generally claim that there is not one word with a number of different meanings, but rather that two or more different words happen to share the same form. It is just a fact about the English language that three separate words all share the form *pen*; linguists sometimes number these separate words to distinguish them from each other: pen$_1$, pen$_2$ and pen$_3$. These three words are described as homonyms; they share the same sound but have completely different meanings and origins.

Context nearly always ensures that the existence of homonyms is not much of a problem. The relevant context can be linguistic, meaning that it is provided by the other words in an utterance, or it can be to do with other aspects of a situation. If someone says to you *I'm off to the bank to pay in this cheque*, you will almost certainly assume that they mean a financial institution rather than the side of a river. If someone holds up a glass containing a red liquid and says *I like a good port* you will assume that they mean fortified wine rather than a harbour. It is quite likely that it will not even occur to you at the time that there are other words with the form *bank* or *port*.

It is not just words that can share a form but have different meanings. Sometimes phrases or whole sentences can be ambiguous. For instance the phrase *Ripe pears and apples* is ambiguous; is it just the pears that are ripe or the apples as well? There are various examples of ambiguous sentences that are much discussed by linguists. One example is *Visiting relatives can be boring*. It is not clear just from looking at this whether it is relatives who come to visit or the act of going to visit relatives that is being described as boring. These cases are referred to as structural ambiguity. We looked briefly at structural ambiguity in Section 2.2 when we considered arguments in support of transformational grammar. Whether or not they agree with Chomsky, linguists generally describe such examples not as one phrase or sentence with more than one meaning, but as two different linguistic structures that result in the same string of words. In the first case there is one phrase in which *ripe* modifies just *pears*, and one in which it modifies both *apples and pears*. In the second case there is one sentence in which the subject, the noun *relatives*, is modified by the adjective *visiting* and one sentence in which the subject is the clause *visiting relatives*.

Ambiguity may not pose much of a threat to communication because of the part played by context in establishing which word or sentence was uttered, but this in itself raises some problems for language theorists. As with deixis, there are apparently cases where context is necessary to determine not just what particular effect speakers mean their words to have, or what extra pieces of meaning are being conveyed, but actually what the literal meaning is of the the words used. Any figurative meaning or illocutionary force can be established only after one of two or more possible literal meanings has been chosen. We might say that context plays a role in establishing what proposition is expressed.

Again there are two distinct reactions to this problem. One is to view ambiguity, like deixis, as evidence that it is not possible to make a straightforward distinction between semantic meaning, which is propositional, and pragmatic meaning, which is to do with intention and force. Some considerations that might seem to belong firmly within pragmatics – such as what would be most relevant to a particular context – are seen to be encroaching on decisions about semantic meaning. Those who maintain that semantics and pragmatics are autonomous argue that context does not actually determine the proposition expressed. A particular word or sentence has been employed by a speaker with a particular meaning, and this does not depend on context. The only role for context is to aid the hearer to establish exactly which proposition is present.

7.6   Further reading

See Jeffries (2006, section 7.4.1) for the multiple meanings of lexical ambiguity and the referential properties of deictic expressions. Clark (2006, chs 2 and 3) has discussions of pragmatics (including speech act theory) and stylistics. Pragmatics developed out of the work by Austin, and uses general, non-linguistic principles to describe the difference between language and language use. Speech act theory has also played a part in the development of some aspects of stylistics.

In the 1950s J. L. Austin put forward his ideas about speech acts, including performatives and his own reservations about them, in a series of lectures called 'How to do Things with Words'. These lectures were published in book form in the 1960s (Austin, 1962). John Searle has written extensively about Austin's ideas and speech acts; one such work is Searle (1969). His ideas about indirect speech acts are presented in Searle (1979). One early philosophical commentary on the relationships between speech act theory and conventional meaning is Strawson (1964). The use of indirectness in everyday speech, and the effect on it of politeness, are discussed extensively in Brown and Levinson (1987).

The idea that context seems to be necessary to resolve issues of deixis and ambiguity, and therefore perhaps to arrive at any complete meaning at all, has been the subject of intense debate in pragmatics for a number of years. The central issue in this debate has been whether the semantics of a language is capable of producing a literal meaning for any sentence, or whether it must interact with pragmatic principles before meaning can be explained. Central texts include Sperber and Wilson (1995), Gazdar (1979), Cole (1981), Horn (1989), Levinson (1983, 2000) and Bach (2001).

Is Language Logical? **8**

CHAPTER 8

8.1 Introduction

When people comment on language, particularly when they talk about what they view as correct usage, they sometimes talk about what is logical. For instance you may have heard criticisms of the use of the double negative on the ground that it does not work logically. In mathematics two negatives cancel each other out and make a positive: $3 - - 5$ is equivalent to $3 + 5$. But in some dialects of English, speakers use two negatives without intending to convey a positive; *I haven't seen nobody* does not mean *I have seen somebody*. Criticisms of such examples on the ground that they are illogical suggest a belief that language is, or at least ought to be, governed by the laws of logic. There is something very appealing about this idea, and indeed it has formed the basis of a considerable amount of work by language theorists. However, as we will see, any straightforward use of logic to explain language quickly runs into problems. The task of the language theorist is then to decide how to deal with these problems.

There are some obvious features of logic that in part explain why it is an appealing candidate to explain language. It employs symbols that stand in for different types of meaning. Specifically there are 'logical constants' (some of which we will consider below) that always mean the same thing. Then there are 'variables': symbols that have different meanings on different occasions. Typically letters such as *p*, *q*, and *r* are used to stand in for any simple proposition. As we saw in Chapter 4, a simple proposition is a single fact or the content of a single thought. Propositions are usually expressed in language by simple declarative sentences, such as *Cardiff is the capital of Wales* or *John is musical*. The logical constants and variables can be combined in different ways to make meaningful statements. Logicians have worked out laws that

127

explain these combinations and how they affect meaning, so it might seem like a good idea to use these same explanations for meaning in language.

Suppose we were to adopt a working hypothesis that meaning in language is equivalent to meaning in logic. We would find plenty of examples that would seem to justify this hypothesis. There are a number of expressions in language that seem to correspond in meaning to elements already explained in logic. For the present purposes we will look just at conjunctions and conditionals. Logical conjunction, as its name suggests, is a way of joining together two or more propositions to form a more complex proposition. The symbol most frequently used for conjunctions is ∧. If true simple propositions are put together you will end up with a true complex proposition. So if p is true and q is true, then $p \land q$ must also be true. Something very similar seems to happen with the word *and*; it can be used to join two statements, and as long as both statements are true you will end up with a further true statement. If *John got into his car* is true and *John drove to Cardiff* is true, then it is true to say that *John got into his car and John drove to Cardiff*, or to express the same complex proposition more naturally, *John got into his car and drove to Cardiff.*

Logical conditionals are represented by the symbol →. These conditionals are often compared to natural language *if . . . then*. In a complex proposition involving a conditional, if the first simple proposition is true then the second one must also be true for the proposition as a whole to be true. If r is a true proposition then $r \to q$ will be true only if q is also true. Similarly if we are confident that *Cardiff is the capital of Wales* is true, we need to establish that *John drove to Cardiff* is true before we can agree that *If Cardiff is the capital of Wales then John drove to Cardiff* is true.

However, once we think a bit more about how expressions such as *and* and *if . . . then* are used, we find that they are perhaps not as close to their logical counterparts as at first appeared. To put this another way, we soon identify some apparent counterexamples to our hypothesis that the meanings of such expressions are explained by the rules of logic. For instance, for a logical conjunction to be true all that is required is that both simple propositions are true. In a mathematical sum the order in which the numbers being added together are placed makes no difference: 3 + 5 is equivalent to 5 + 3. In the same way, in the case of logical conjunction $p \land q$ is equivalent to $q \land p$. This is where the first problem arises for our hypothesis that meaning in language is equivalent to meaning in logic. We have established that if *John got into his car* and *John drove to Cardiff* are both true, then *John got into his car and drove to Cardiff* must also be true. But in this case the order in which we present the facts is significant. We would probably not be as happy to accept *John drove to Cardiff and got into his car*. Even if we did not judge it to be false, we would probably think that there was something odd or misleading about it. It certainly seems to be telling us something rather different from the earlier way of describing the same events. So this example and many others like it present problems for our hypothesis that *and* is explained by ∧. In the case of *and*, but not of ∧, the order in which the events are presented does seem to be significant. In particular we expect the event that occurred first to be the one that is described first.

Things start to look even worse for our hypothesis when we consider *if . . . then* in more detail. Again the meaning of the logical constant → is defined simply in terms of truth: if *p*, *q* and *r* are all true then the complex propositions *r* → *q*, *q* → *r*, *p* → *r* and so on are also true. But *if . . . then* does not appear to be so flexible. We might be happy with *If Cardiff is the capital of Wales then John drove to Cardiff*, but that does not mean that we would also accept *If John drove to Cardiff then Cardiff is the capital of Wales*. And certainly *If John got into his car then Cardiff is the capital of Wales* would generally be judged as extremely odd indeed. It seems that *if . . . then* raises expectations that there is some link, or relevance, between the two events described, expectations that are not associated with the logical →.

For many language theorists the problems associated with trying to explain language in terms of logic are just too grave. Many philosophers of language have argued that language cannot be described in terms of logic. Broadly speaking, philosophers fall into one of two groups, depending on how they explain this. We will consider each explanation in turn, and then look at what happened when two philosophers, one from each group, argued about a particular type of relationship between logic and language. After that we will look at a different theoretical approach to the problem: the assertion that there is not such a big difference between logic and language after all.

8.2   'Natural language is messy and imperfect'

Philosophers in the first group are sometimes labelled 'formalists'. This is a different use of the term from that used to describe formalist linguists, who are concerned with the structures and rules rather than the communicative use of language. Formalist philosophers are so-called because they are interested in formal or rule-governed logic. They are not a unified group; they have worked at different times and in different philosophical traditions, and they would certainly have disagreed on many points. But they have shared a response to the problems we have identified, which can be summarised informally as: 'It's no wonder that language doesn't fit the rules of logic; natural language is messy and imperfect'. Formalists have pointed to the differences between language and logic such as those we have just considered, as well as some other ways in which natural language lacks precision and clarity. They have tended to argue that it is best for philosophers to steer clear of natural language, with all its problems and inconsistencies, and concentrate instead on logical languages, which are artificially constructed and therefore fit for the purpose. Some of the most influential philosophers to take this position were the logical positivists of the Vienna Circle, whose work on 'verificationism' we considered in Chapter 4. The logical positivists argued that natural language was not good enough for scientific description or for philosophy because it was inconsistent and illogical. Here is a passage from the work of Rudolf Carnap, a member of the Vienna Circle:

> In consequence of the unsystematic and logically imperfect structure of the natural word-languages (such as German or Latin), the statement of their formal rules of formation and transformation would be so complicated that it would hardly be feasible in practice . . . Instead, we shall consider the syntax of two artificially constructed symbolic languages (that is to say, such languages as employ formal symbols instead of words). As a matter of fact, throughout all modern logical investigations, this is the method used; for only in a symbolic language has it proved possible to achieve exact formulation and rigid proofs (Carnap, 1937, pp. 2–3).

This is a clear statement from Carnap that what he called the 'natural word-languages' – languages spoken by ordinary people for their everyday purposes – were not up to the job when it came to formal philosophy. He proposed to replace these natural word languages with an artificial language carefully constructed for the purpose. Another fairly common claim from formalists was that if natural language was going to be referred to in philosophical discussions it should first be 'cleaned up' by removing its problematic inconsistencies. Natural language was full of expressions that were vague or unclear, and the job of the philosopher was to translate these into more precise, philosophical terms: to show what our words really meant, despite misleading appearances. An example of a formalist who made this claim was A. J. Ayer, the British philosopher who introduced the ideas of the Vienna Circle to the English-speaking world. This is how he put it:

> We find that in all sentences of the form 'p is true', the phrase 'is true' is logically superfluous. When, for example, one says that the proposition 'Queen Anne is dead' is true, all that one is saying is that Queen Anne is dead. And similarly, when one says that the proposition 'Oxford is the capital of England' is false, all that one is saying is that Oxford is not the capital of England. Thus, to say that a proposition is true is just to assert it, and to say that it is false is just to assert its contradictory. And this indicates that the terms 'true' and 'false' connote nothing, but function

in the sentence simply as marks of assertion and denial. And in that case there can be no sense in asking us to analyse the concept of 'truth' (Ayer, 1971, p. 118).

Ayer was claiming that when sloppy natural language was translated into rigorous philosophical language some expressions, such as *is true*, had no meaning at all. Therefore whatever people said in their everyday use of language, such expressions should not appear in the language of philosophy. Language needed to be tidied up by removing such meaningless expressions before it could be used for philosophical analysis.

8.3 'Logic is the wrong tool for the job'

Some of the strongest criticisms levelled at formalists have been in response to their attitude towards natural language. Theorists who have disagreed with them have argued that it is not right, indeed it is not possible, to dismiss natural language from consideration on the grounds that it is messy and illogical. They have suggested that if language does not fit the patterns of logic, this is simply because logic is not the best system for explaining language. Rather than dismissing language from philosophical discussions, it is better to get rid of the idea that logical explanations are always the best, and to find a more appropriate system for describing and explaining language. After all there is no reason why a system devised for the purposes of mathematics and science should be expected to be a useful tool for discussing natural systems of human communication.

This type of criticism was voiced particularly strongly by the group of 'ordinary language philosophers' that included J. L. Austin, who was the founder of speech act theory. As we saw in the previous chapter, Austin argued that ordinary, natural language was a valid topic for philosophical study in its own right. Indeed it was necessary for philosophers to study language carefully because it was a system, built up and refined over generations, that people used to describe their experience and understanding of the world. If philosophers ignored natural language they were in danger of missing out on all this experience and understanding, and perhaps of being misled by artificial philosophical language. Austin argued that philosophers who devised formal languages into which to translate everyday expressions were doing little more than thinking up new forms of expression in isolation from experience and from contact with other people. As such they were almost bound to fall into error and confusion.

Because they valued natural language over formal logical language, the philosophers of ordinary language were particularly scathing about attempts to explain language in terms of logic, and to criticise language when it failed to meet the standards that this imposed. Another ordinary language philosopher, Gilbert Ryle, wrote about what he described as the 'formaliser's dream': the desire to translate natural language into logical notation for the purposes of rigorous philosophical analysis. Some of the opponents of this position, he suggested:

> maintain that the logic of the statements of scientists, lawyers, historians and bridge-players cannot in principle be adequately represented by the formulae of formal logic. The so-called logical constants do indeed have, partly by deliberate prescription, their scheduled logical powers; but the non-formal expressions both of everyday discourse and of technical discourse have their own unscheduled logical powers, and these are not reducible without remainder to those of the carefully wired marionettes of formal logic (Ryle, 1963, p. 125).

This is a difficult passage, but it is possible to see in it Ryle's main objections to the formalists. His use of the 'marionettes' metaphor in the final sentence provides a clue. Ryle was arguing that logic could offer only a highly artificial, simplified picture of the meaning of language, just as a puppet was an artificial and simplified representation of a human being. It was just not possible to describe meaning in terms of logic, or at least to do so 'without remainder'. In other words there would always be aspects of meaning left over, unexplained, after logic had been used, because natural meaning was more complex and more subtle than logic.

8.4   Focus on Russell *versus* Strawson

There is another possible response to the failure of the hypothesis that logic can explain the meaning of language, one that disagrees with both the formalists and the informalists. We will look at this alternative response soon, but first it will be interesting to spend a little time thinking about what happened when one formalist theorist and an informalist theorist disagreed about how to explain a particular type of meaning. We will briefly consider a written debate that took place in the early and middle years of the twentieth century between the philosophers Bertrand Russell and Peter Strawson. Russell was an early proponent of the so-called analytic approach to philosophy. According to this approach language should be subjected to rigorous logical analysis and if necessary expressions from natural language should be translated into clearer, more logically precise forms for the purposes of philosophy. He was therefore a formalist in his approach. Strawson was a philosopher of ordinary language. Although he disagreed with Austin on various matters, he shared the basic beliefs that natural language was a legitimate topic for philosophy in its own right, and that it was inappropriate to try to make it fit pre-existing ideas about logic. He therefore took a broadly informalist approach, arguing that logic was not the right tool for the analysis of language. The debate between them is interesting because it brings out clearly the differences between these two approaches. It also raises some important questions about a particular type of meaning in natural language, and offers two different answers to those questions.

The questions were raised by Russell in an article he published in 1905. In this he discussed some apparently straightforward examples in which a particular individual was said to have a certain property, for instance *The prime minister of Britain is tall*. This contains what is known as a 'denoting expression'; the expression *The prime minister of England* denotes, or picks out, a particular individual in the world. It appears to function in very much the same way as a proper name. As we saw in Chapter 3, part of the meaning of a name or expression is generally claimed to be its extension, or the individual in the world to which it refers. In these terms *the prime minister of Britain is tall* and *Tony Blair is tall* mean the same thing (in 2006). In the usual terminology of grammatical analysis we would describe this sentence as consisting of a noun phrase subject, *The prime minister of Britain* and a verb phrase predicate, *is tall*, where the predicate tells us something about the subject. In the terminology of logic we have just been using, we could say that the sentence expresses the simple proposition, *p*, that the prime minister of Britain is tall.

It seems reasonable to suggest that if we want to find out whether *p* is true or false we need only look at the relevant piece of evidence: look at the prime minister of Britain and decide whether or not he is tall. However Russell argued that the analysis of sentences of this type was not as straightforward as it might at first appear because of a problem with the analysis of denoting expressions. To see why, consider a sentence such as Russell's own example 'the king of France is bald'. Following on from what we have just said, this looks as though it is a sentence of subject-predicate form, expressing a simple proposition. The problem is that there has been no king of France since 1848. The phrase *the king of France* does not pick out any individual in the world to which the property *bald* can be attributed; the sentence as a whole is not 'about' anyone or anything. Russell pointed out that this ought to mean that the sentence was simply nonsense, but that this was not the case; he claimed that 'the king of France is bald' did make sense, but was obviously false.

Russell put forward an idea that suggests a solution to this problem, but only at the expense of translating these simple-looking sentences into much more complex logical forms. He argued that they were not actually of subject-predicate form at all. The assumption that they were was the result of their misleading appearance. For Russell these sentences provided examples of how natural language was imprecise and of how the philosopher needed to be on guard against this, and to be prepared to think about logic rather than language when necessary. In the following passage Russell set out his version of the correct, or logical, meaning of sentences of this sort. He was discussing the example 'the author of *Waverley* was a man', but what he said can be applied equally to any sentences of this type:

> According to the view which I advocate, a denoting phrase is essentially *part* of a sentence, and does not, like most single words, have any significance on its own account. If I say 'Scott was a man,' that is a statement of the form 'x was a man,' and it has 'Scott' for its subject. But if I say 'the author of *Waverley* was a man,' that is not a statement of the form 'x was man,' and does not have 'the author of *Waverley*' for its subject . . . we may put, in place of 'the author of *Waverley* was a man,' the following: 'One and only one entity wrote *Waverley*, and that one was a man' . . . And speaking generally, suppose we wish to say that the author of *Waverley* had the property Φ, what we wish to say is equivalent to 'One and only one entity wrote *Waverley*, and that one had the property Φ' (Russell, 1905, p. 488).

So Russell was drawing a distinction between sentences introduced by proper names and those introduced by denoting phrases. The first did consist of a subject and a predicate, as they seemed to, but the second did not. Elsewhere in the article Russell argued that denoting phrases that began with *the* were a special case because they did not just pick out an individual, they also introduced the idea that the individual existed and was unique. If this idea of uniqueness was not required the phrases would be *an author of Waverley* or *a king of France*. Russell believed that the logical form of a sentence must spell out all the aspects of meaning that the sentence conveyed, even if its grammatical form was deficient in this respect. Therefore the meanings of such sentences were not simple but complex propositions. The sentence 'the king of France is bald' should be understood as having, or must be translated to reveal, the logical form $p \land q \land r$ where p is the proposition *There is an entity which is king of France*, q is the proposition *That entity is unique* and r is the proposition *That entity is bald*. In this way Russell offered a solution to the problem he had identified that the sentence should by rights be meaningless but was in fact simply false. Logic tells us that a complex proposition made up of the conjunction of a number of simple propositions is false if any one of those simple propositions is false. Since there is no king of France, p is false, and therefore $p \land q \land r$ is false.

Strawson's response to what became known as 'Russell's theory of descriptions' was published in an article in 1950. Strawson's central criticism was that

Russell, like many other formalists, was so obsessed with formal logic that he tried to apply it to the topic of human communication where it just did not belong. Because formal logic worked well in one field, namely mathematics, Russell had assumed that it could equally well be applied to a completely different field. Formalist approaches such as Russell's concentrated on possible logical analyses of particular expressions and sentences, while ignoring the fact that such expressions and sentences generally occurred when they were used in context by speakers. Strawson argued that, instead of making the formalist assumption that every statement was either true or false, and therefore that 'the king of France is bald' must be false since it was not true, it would be better to consider how you would react if you actually heard the sentence in use. If you did this, he suggested, you would realise that you would not respond 'That's false!', but rather would be unsure as to how to respond at all, sensing that something very odd had just been said. It might be necessary to point out that the speaker must be making a mistake: there is no king of France.

> And this brings out the point that if a man seriously uttered the sentence, his uttering it would in some sense be *evidence* that he *believed* that there was a king of France . . . We might put it as follows. To say 'The king of France is wise' is, in some sense of 'imply', to *imply* that there is a king of France. But this is a very special and odd sense of 'imply' . . . And this comes out from the fact that when, in response to his statement, we say (as we should) 'There is no king of France', we should certainly *not* say we were *contradicting* the statement that the king of France is wise. We are certainly not saying that it's false. We are, rather, giving a reason for saying that the question of whether it's true or false simply doesn't arise (Strawson, 1950, p. 330).

According to Strawson, then, there was no need to put forward a complex translation of the sentence in which a commitment to the existence of the king of France was part of the proposition expressed. Rather, any use of the sentence carried that commitment as a particular type of implication. Strawson did not give this type of implication a name in this article, but in later work he described it as 'presupposition', and this name has stuck in philosophy and linguistics. A presupposition is a necessary starting point for a statement to be either true or false. To put this another way, you need to establish that the king of France exists before you can start a meaningful discussion of whether or not he is bald. *There is a king of France* must be true before either *The king of France is bald* or *The king of France is not bald* can be used meaningfully, let alone truly.

It is probably unnecessary to add that no agreement was ever reached between Russell and Strawson. They were approaching the problems posed by examples such as 'the king of France' from different theoretical backgrounds and with different assumptions about language. Russell's aim was to solve a particular problem presented by language in such a way that the laws and expectations of formal logic could be upheld, and if necessary to do so by explaining the errors and irregularities of natural language. As such his theory might be considered a great success. Strawson was urging theorists to abandon their preoccupation with logic and start paying attention to language as a system of communication. And in these terms his theory, which took account of how people reacted to the use of sentences in everyday situations and explained something about how communication worked, was also successful. Russell and Strawson made very different claims. In fact their theories were incompatible with each other, not least because Russell's theory depended on his judgment that 'the king of France is bald' was false, while Strawson's theory depended on its being neither true nor false. But the fact that we are not in a position to decide conclusively which of them was right in this matter is really not significant. They both had some interesting ideas about what language is and about how it relates to logic.

8.5   'Logic can't do the whole job by itself'

Not all theorists who think about the relationship between logic and language take either a formalist or an informalist position. There is one approach that disagrees with both these traditions and suggests a different type of explanation. It has its origins in Paul Grice's work on conversational implicature (see for example Grice, 1975, 1989). If you are familiar with Grice's work you may be surprised to find it turning up in a discussion of logic. His ideas on conversational implicature are often explained in textbooks on pragmatics or discourse analysis. They have provided the starting point for thinking about the way that conversations work, and for studies that analyse different types of language use. This might all seem a far remove from the question of whether language is logical. However it is possible to think about Grice's ideas in a way that makes them highly relevant to the issues we are considering here.

Grice claims that it is possible to identify some regularities in the way in which information is exchanged in conversation. Although they may not always be consciously aware of it, participants in a conversation follow certain rational patterns of behaviour, and have the expectation that the people they are talking to do will do the same. The patterns of behaviour in question all follow from a general expectation that conversation is a collaborative activity: that as far as possible participants will work together towards the successful exchange of information. Grice's 'cooperative principle' states that participants produce the most appropriate contribution at any given stage in a conversation. This principle is backed up by four categories of maxim that specify what it is that makes a contribution appropriate. Briefly, the category of quantity states that participants should give neither more nor less information than is appropriate; the category of quality states that they should give only information that they believe to be true; the category of relation states that the information should be relevant; and the category of manner states that it should be presented in an orderly way.

The expectation that people are observing the maxims included in these categories can explain how a lot of meaning in conversation is conveyed by suggestion, or in Grice's terminology is implicated, rather than being stated explicitly. To use one of Grice's examples, imagine that you are standing next to your car by the side of the road, a stranger stops to offer help, and you say 'I am out of petrol'. The stranger replies 'There is a garage round the corner'. The stranger has not actually told you that the garage in question is the type that sells petrol, but you would probably assume this was meant. After all it would be extremely unhelpful, or uncooperative, of the stranger to tell you about the garage while knowing that it only did servicing and repairs. So while the literal meaning (or for Grice, what is said), is simply that there is a garage around the corner, the implied meaning (or for Grice, what is implicated), is that the garage sells petrol. You derive this on the reasonable assumption that the stranger is being cooperative and in particular is observing the expectation of relevance. It is a conversational implicature of what the stranger said.

Grice's theory has been a success in pragmatics and discourse analysis because of the potential it offers for explaining how meaning is conveyed in a wide range of conversational settings. However because of this success Grice's original intentions tend to be overlooked. He originally put forward his ideas in a series of lectures called 'Logic and Conversation'. He made it clear towards the start of these that one of his main interests was the relationship between logic and language. Conversation was a topic he had been thinking about in order to explain this relationship. Grice discussed the debate about logic that we have been considering: the debate between formalists and informalists. Both groups agreed that there were significant divergences between logic and language; the difference between them was how they reacted to these divergences. Grice explained that he would not be taking sides with either group:

> I wish, rather, to maintain that the common assumption of the contestants that the divergences do in fact exist is (broadly speaking) a common mistake, and that the mistake arises from inadequate attention to the nature and importance of the conditions governing conversation. I shall,

therefore, inquire into the general conditions that, in one way or another, apply to conversation as such, irrespective of its subject matter (Grice, 1975, p. 24).

This was a surprising contribution to the debate. Grice was proposing to demonstrate that the whole disagreement between formalists and informalists was based on a mistake. There were no divergences between logic and language. Furthermore both sides had made this mistake because they had not taken enough account of the regularities of conversation. We might well ask how Grice could make such rash claims, given the differences between logic and language we looked at at the start of this chapter. His claims relied on the argument that when theorists looked at meaning in language they looked only at the whole of what was conveyed in any particular context, overlooking the fact that there might be a distinction between what was literally said and what was merely implicated. The theory of conversation, and the maxims that accounted for how people interacted and understood each other, could explain away the apparent differences between logic and language, leaving the system of logic as a clear-cut and useful way of explaining meaning.

To illustrate Grice's point we can turn again to the examples of the apparent differences between logic and language with which we began this chapter. Remember that if natural language *and* meant the same as logical ∧ then we ought to find that *John got into his car and drove to Cardiff* and *John drove to Cardiff and got into his car* are exactly the same in meaning, yet this does not seem to be the case. In most contexts we would probably find the first version perfectly acceptable, but the second distinctly odd. But suppose that the literal meaning of *and* is in fact the same as the logical conjunction ∧; this is what is said whenever someone says *and*. Then those extra meanings, such as the suggestion that the events have occurred in the order in which they are expressed, could be explained as conversational implicatures associated with the use of the word. In particular the expectation that what people say will be presented in an orderly manner encourages us to assume that the order in which events are presented was the order in which they actually occurred. This explains why, in the most likely situation that John got into his car first and then drove to Cardiff, we would find the second example particularly odd or misleading, even if we were grudgingly to admit that it was literally true. It is odd because although what is said is strictly true, it is expressed in such a way as to introduce an implicature that does not correspond to reality.

A similar explanation can be found for the apparent differences between *if . . . then* and the logical conditional →. Remember that logic would not be able to tell us why *If Cardiff is the capital of Wales then John drove to Cardiff* seems a reasonable thing to say, while *If John got into his car then Cardiff is the capital of Wales* seems distinctly odd. In natural language we expect some sort of connection between the two parts of an *if . . . then* sentence, perhaps some explanation as to why our knowledge of the second part is dependent on our knowledge of the first part. Grice suggests that we could understand this expectation as an implicature associated with the use of an *if . . . then* sentence in conversation. What is said when you use an *if . . . then* sentence may well be equivalent to a logical conditional, but there is also an implicature of some sort of relevance or cause and effect. This follows from our expectation that people will not say more than they have reason to believe; if you simply mean that two events happen, it would be more cooperative to use a simple conjunction.

We can now explain the differences in acceptability between our examples. We can accept *If Cardiff is the capital of Wales then John drove to Cardiff* because the implicature of relevance seems reasonable. We can imagine a context in which knowledge of the second part depends on knowledge of the first; perhaps someone knows that John drove to the capital of Wales, but is not sure whether the capital of Wales is Cardiff. *If John got into his car then Cardiff is the capital of Wales* seems odd because it is not easy to detect any relevance between the two pieces of information. It is hard to imagine why someone's knowledge of what is the capital of Wales could depend on their knowledge of what John did. At best you could find yourself trying to think up some pretty unusual contexts that might make this an acceptable thing to say.

A similar explanation can be applied to a number of other apparent discrepancies between logic and language. In another article Grice (1981) suggests that his theory of conversational implicature is useful for examining the debate between Russell and Strawson on denoting phrases and presupposition. He suggests that Russell's logical approach was basically correct, but that Strawson made some important observations about how people generally react to uses of sentences such as 'the king of France is bald'. What is needed is an account of how the form of words chosen presents some parts of information as more likely to be denied than others. There is an implicature that the person you are talking to will accept some parts of your message without complaint, even if she or he may want to challenge others. In this case the existence of the king of France is not presented as something that anyone is going to challenge, explaining Strawson's reaction that it is a presupposition.

In each case Grice's notion of conversational implicature enables him to argue that there is not much difference between logic and language after all. This means that he does not have to accept the formalists' belief that language is messy and not fit for rigorous analysis. Language does have regularities and can be explained systematically; it is just that the explanation cannot be couched entirely in terms of logic. Nor does Grice have to agree with the informalists. Logic can be a useful tool for explaining meaning in language; it is just that it cannot do the whole job by itself. Additional rules to do with how language is used in conversation are needed for a full explanation. Much of the discipline of pragmatics follows from Grice's work on conversation. There are many different pragmatic theories, but they all share a basic premise that it is useful, and possible, to distinguish between formal linguistic meaning and what speakers mean in context, which may be affected by other types of principle.

8.6 Further reading

See Jeffries (2006) for a discussion of the ways in which information is structured by syntactic choices. Oπ2   140
ne way in which distinctions between what is asserted and what is presupposed are discussed in present day linguistics. Jeffries also provides an account of the operation of Grice's cooperative principle in conversation. Clark (2006, ch. 2) includes a discussion of pragmatics in general and Grice's theory of conversational implicature in particular.

The debate between Russell and Strawson took place mainly in two articles: Russell (1905) and Strawson (1950). There are a number of commentaries on and discussions of this debate and its implications, including Martin (1987, ch. 13), Devitt and Sterelny (1988, ch. 3), Stainton (1996, ch. 3) and Chapman (2000, ch. 2).

Grice's theory of conversational implicature is set out in a number of articles, most significantly in Grice (1975). He discusses its implications for the analysis of *if . . . then* sentences in Grice (1989), and for the debate between Russell and Strawson in Grice (1981). There are numerous introductions to and discussions of Grice's work, but these tend to concentrate mainly on conversational implicature. One that emphasises its significance to debates on logic and natural language is McCawley (1993). This book also provides a thorough introduction to the relationship between language and logic more generally, as do Allwood *et al.* (1979). Chapman (2005) considers Grice's work as a whole.

How do Children Learn Language?

9.1 Introduction

Anyone who has learnt a language as an adult knows that it can be a long and difficult process. It is not even always successful. The phrase 'a flair for languages' reflects the view that some people have a particular ability to learn new languages, while others are doomed to struggle and perhaps to fail. Yet everyone succeeds fully in mastering a language at least once. Everyone learns what is variously described as their first language, their native language or their mother tongue. This process of learning takes place during the very early years of childhood, with equal success among children from widely different social, cultural and linguistic backgrounds. It is a topic of enduring interest and some considerable controversy in linguistic theory. This is not least because, like the other issues we have been considering, the question of how children learn language inevitably raises further questions about the nature of language itself.

In this chapter we will look at some of the ways in which the process of learning a first language, or language acquisition as it is often described, has been explained. As we will see, these explanations draw on assumptions about the nature of language of the type discussed in Part I. These assumptions are sometimes implicit in what theorists have said about language acquisition and are sometimes made explicit. Indeed in some cases the relationship to the nature of language itself is the main focus and motivation for work on language acquisition.

9.1 Learning as imitation

One way of learning any new skill is to watch people who already have that skill and imitate what they do, until with practice you too become proficient.

Many theorists of language argue that this is how first language learning takes place. The language being spoken in the community in which a child is growing up provides a model for the child to follow in his or her own attempts. Of course this claim about how language is learnt depends on particular assumptions about what language is in the first place. It depends on seeing language as primarily a set of practical skills, or an ability to behave in certain appropriate ways.

Not surprisingly theorists such as Leonard Bloomfield (1935) and W. V. O. Quine (1960) who, as we saw in Part I, described language as a type of behaviour, explained language learning in terms of imitation. Quine, for instance, described a child as being like a traveller to a remote part of the world who has to try to communicate in a new language with no interpreter. Like the traveller, the child observes the circumstances in which people seem to use particular expressions and tries using those expressions in similar circumstances. Gradually the child develops the tendency to use all the expressions of the language in the same types of circumstance as do the adult speakers of the language. The child has successfully acquired the language.

This account of the process and the successful outcome of language acquisition, like much of Quine's work, owes a lot to behaviourism. As we saw in Part I, the psychological theory of behaviourism had a big impact on the ideas about language put forward by a number of theorists working in the middle part of the twentieth century. Perhaps the best-known attempt to apply behaviourism to the study of language was the book *Verbal Behavior* by B. F. Skinner. This was published in 1957, but Skinner had taken a long time to write it and the ideas he discussed dated right back to the 1930s. Skinner was an experimental psychologist; much of his work involved observing and trying to control the behaviour of laboratory animals. His work has now fallen in to some disrepute, especially among linguists. He is accused of taking explanations that worked well enough for simple patterns of behaviour among rats and pigeons, and trying to use these to account for the much more complex behaviour exhibited by human beings. In fact, in *Verbal Behavior* he wrote very little about laboratory animals. Rather he provided a long, discursive account of how behaviourism could explain the acquisition and use of language, with lots of anecdotes and quotations from literature.

In one passage where Skinner did discuss animal behaviour he explained the process by which a pigeon was trained to walk in a figure of eight. The scientist did not expect the pigeon to learn the required behaviour immediately, or even quickly. To begin with all movement was rewarded with food. Gradually the scientist rewarded only specific types of movement. Reward followed only movement in a particular direction, then only movement in a circle, and eventually movement that completed the full figure of eight. The pigeon eventually learnt the complex behaviour of walking in a figure of eight because this became the only behaviour that resulted in a reward. Skinner explained that the relevance of all this was that in the very early stages of language learning children are not expected to produce fully recognisable sentences, words or even speech sounds. To being with almost anything will do. Adults react enthusiastically to anything the child produces that is even remotely like a sound in the language. Skinner explained this process using the terminology of behaviourism:

> In teaching the young child to talk, the formal specifications upon which reinforcement is contingent are at first greatly relaxed. Any response which vaguely resembles the standard behavior of the community is reinforced. When these begin to appear frequently, a closer approximation is insisted upon. In this manner very complex verbal forms may be reached (Skinner, 1957, pp. 29–30).

The child learns very complex patterns of behaviour gradually over time, just as the pigeon gradually learns to walk in a figure of eight. Initially no particular stimulus or trigger in the environment is required. The child produces sounds spontaneously. Sounds that approximate to speech sounds in the language are reinforced by praise and enthusiasm from the adults around, so the child becomes progressively more likely to produce those sounds and less likely to produce other random sounds.

As the child progresses from individual sounds to words and then sentences, aspects of the environment start to become relevant as stimuli that prompt speech. For instance the child sees a doll and produces the utterance *doll*. The child is thirsty and produces the utterance *milk*. At the same time the types of reinforcement become more complex. The child's attempts at speech result not just in attention and praise but also have more specific consequences. The child who utters *doll* is handed the toy, while the child who utters *milk* is given a drink. As a result they are more likely to produce these utterances in future when similar stimuli present themselves. The child learns to behave in a way similar to the adults around through a process of conditioning.

Skinner claimed that it was perfectly possible for the whole pattern of behaviour that we know as a language to be learnt and then used in this way. Of course the stimuli would often be more complex than the sight of a doll or the sensation of thirst, and the reinforcements would often be more complex than being handed a toy or given a drink. We might be stimulated by the desire to influence other people or to work out a complex problem. The relevant stimulus might not always be easy to identify. It might depend on complex aspects of our experience in the recent or even distant past. Just because it was not always easy to identify a particular stimulus in the immediate environment, this did not mean that no stimulus was in effect. Similarly people might be reinforced by the approval and admiration they received as a result of what they said or by success in getting what they wanted. Skinner also suggested that writers could be reinforced in their behaviour by an expectation of how their work would be received in the future, and that people could 'self-reinforce' their behaviour by being pleased with something they had said. In all cases, he argued, language worked according to a basic pattern of stimulus, response and reinforcement.

The complex pattern of behaviour that was built up is what Skinner described as the 'verbal repertoire' of an individual. This included all the vocabulary that an individual had the capacity to use in appropriate circumstances, together with the capacity to combine this vocabulary in various ways to form longer utterances. There were various 'frames' into which words could fit. Initially children learnt simple sentences just as they learnt single words: as single responses to particular stimuli:

> From such behavior there eventually emerges a basic repertoire of smaller functional units also at the level of the word. The child who has acquired the responses *I have a doll* and *I have a kitten* upon separate occasions may show some functional unity in the expression *I have a . . .* which is later combined with novel responses under novel circumstances – for example, when the child says for the first time, and without separate conditioning, *I have a drum* (ibid., p. 119).

Skinner's account of how language was learnt and how it operated was of course based on his belief that language was a type of behaviour. He put this point of view across very explicitly and even described language as a 'muscular movement', emphasising that all that could be talked about when discussing language was the individual physical behaviour of speakers. Words, sentences and language itself did not exist apart from that behaviour. So Skinner emphasised that he had set himself the entirely empirical, even practical, task of describing and explaining one type of human behaviour. His book was not theoretical because 'It makes no appeal to hypothetical explanatory entities' (ibid., p. 12).

Skinner made it clear that he saw language as being just like any other type of human behaviour, and therefore that it should be described in the same way. To isolate language from other types of behaviour for discussion in his book was in many ways an artificial process, but one that he had undertaken for the sake of clarity, to shed some light on this particularly interesting type of behaviour. Skinner's term 'verbal behavior' included not just what we might traditionally recognise as language, but behaviour as diverse as knocking on a door to be let in, clapping at the end of a concert to show appreciation and putting a finger to your lips to request silence. For Skinner these were all types of behaviour that functioned to alter the behaviour of others, and therefore there was no real difference between them.

9.3 Focus on Chomsky's response to Skinner

Noam Chomsky, whose mentalist account of language we considered in Part I, disagreed strongly with behaviourist accounts of language. He did not actually cause behaviourism to be abandoned, but it was probably in part because of him that it fell into disrepute, at least in relation to the study of language. It is rare for a review of a book to be remembered much after it has been published, but Chomsky's review of Skinner's *Verbal Behavior* in the journal *Language* (Chomsky, 1959) is still referred to today. This is because Chomsky used this review not just to comment on Skinner's book, but also to put forward some of his own alternative ideas about language acquisition, and about language more generally.

Chomsky argued that the notion of 'reinforcement', which may have had some success in explaining the behaviour of animals in a laboratory, could not be extended to explain the use of language by speakers. Skinner had only managed to do so by stretching the notion of reinforcement to cover so many different types of experience that it had lost its original meaning. Explaining language in terms of reinforcement could not work because the circumstances in which it was used were just too diverse and complex. Language itself was also much more sophisticated than any type of behaviour observed in laboratory animals. It was more complex than Skinner assumed in his account of sentences being composed by picking appropriate words and putting them into grammatical sequences, or 'frames'. Chomsky gave a number of examples in support of this claim. *Furiously sleep ideas green colorless* and *Friendly young dogs seem harmless* had the same frame but one was a grammatical sentence of English while the other was grammatical only if read from back to front. *Struggling artists can be a nuisance* and *Marking papers can be a nuisance* had the same frame but very different sentence structures. Chomsky concluded from these examples that:

> It is evident that more is involved in sentence structure than insertion of lexical items in grammatical frames; no approach to language that fails to take these deeper processes into account can possibly achieve much success in accounting for actual linguistic behavior (Chomsky, 1959, p. 54).

So Chomsky rejected Skinner's account of language learning and prepared to put forward his own account. The passage above points towards the views we considered in Section 2.2: that language is a complex, structured system in which both phrase structure and transformational rules contribute to the construction of sentences. Elsewhere in his review Chomsky referred to the complexity of speakers. Skinner's account of language dwelt on the environmental factors that acted on language users, but it was curiously silent about the nature of language users themselves: about what Chomsky called their 'internal structure'. That is, the behaviourist account of language had nothing to say about the mental processes in which speakers were involved. Chomsky continued:

> Insofar as independent neurological evidence is not available, it is obvious that inferences concerning the structure of the organism are based on observation of behavior and outside events. Nevertheless, one's estimate of the relative importance of external factors and internal structure in the determination of behavior will have an important effect on the direction of research on linguistic (or any other) behavior, and on the kinds of analogies from animal behavior studies that will be considered relevant or suggestive (ibid., p. 27).

The internal structure that for Chomsky was so important was not available for direct study; a researcher could not see people's minds. Instead the behaviour of people in their environment was all that the researcher had to go on. But while Skinner thought that this was the only thing the researcher should concentrate on, for Chomsky it was just a starting point. From observations about behaviour and the environment the researcher could draw inferences or reach conclusions about what must be going on inside the organism in question: in this case the language user. Chomsky drew attention to the link between views on language and methods of linguistic research. Researchers' view on the relative importance of internal and external factors would determine how their investigation of language would proceed. If, like Skinner, researchers assumed that external factors were of prime importance, they would study only these. However, if like Chomsky they believed that language could not be explained without reference to internal or mental features, they would use the study of external phenomena simply as a starting point.

This belief that an account of language must include reference to internal features of language users remained a constant theme in Chomsky's work. Many of his subsequent writings were concerned with the exact nature of those features. In his review of *Verbal Behavior* he was remarkably cautious about suggesting what they might consist of. He drew attention to some of the complexities of language that had been overlooked by Skinner, and the fact that children almost always succeeded in fully acquiring all this complex knowledge. He then proposed that evidence of this sort pointed to the conclusion that 'human beings are somehow specially designed to do this, with data-handling or "hypothesis-formulating" ability of unknown character and complexity' (ibid., p. 57).

The reference to 'special design' is the vital clue to what came next in Chomsky's thinking. As we saw in Section 2.2, he developed the idea that the ability to acquire and then to use language was an essential and in-built part of human nature, that it was an innate feature of human minds. According to Chomsky's innateness hypothesis (IH), far from being learnt on the basis of observation, imitation and memory, language develops in a human being at a biologically determined point in early childhood. It is not learnt, as riding a bicycle is learnt, but develops naturally, as walking develops naturally. The child needs exposure to language use in order to learn the vocabulary and the specific local features of the particular language in question. But the general structures that underlie all human languages, and the ability to build on these in order to acquire a particular human language, are preprogrammed. Like many other innate features, the language faculty is triggered at a particular stage in the child's development. It also seems to close off after a certain length of time, leaving a critical period in which language acquisition can take place. Somewhere around puberty people seem to lose the ability to acquire language naturally and effortlessly, explaining the problems encountered by adult learners that we considered at the start of this chapter.

Chomsky was therefore refuting not just behaviourism, which was after all a rather narrow target, but any description of language as dependent on general learning mechanisms. His later claims about what was innate became much more specific than his early reference to data-handling. He proposed that the type of knowledge involved in language was so complex and so specialised that there must be an innate ability concerned just with this: an innate language faculty.

The arguments that Chomsky put forward in support of the IH included some of the features of his theory of language that we looked at in Section 2.2: for instance that similarities across languages pointed to a universal grammar that could be present in all human minds only if it was part of our genetic endowment. In response to the idea of language learning as imitation, Chomsky's most significant argument was his description of the 'poverty of stimulus'. This was the claim that the way in which people ordinarily use language is just too messy, faulty and imperfect to facilitate the complex linguistic knowledge that children acquire. The way in which people use language in their everyday interactions, and therefore the evidence about the language available to children, is full of ungrammaticalities, hesitations and false starts. Children only ever encounter performance in which competence interacts with factors that have nothing at all to do with language, and which is therefore full of performance errors. It is also necessarily incomplete because children will only ever encounter a finite amount of performance but the number of possible sentences of a language is infinite. This gives rise to the logical problem of language acquisition. The input alone cannot explain the output, or children's successful progression to the steady state of linguistic knowledge. Therefore there must be certain features of the initial state, the mental properties that children are born with, that resolve this problem.

The initial state must include outlines of types of grammatical rules that need only be triggered by exposure to a little data from language use to produce full linguistic competence. That is, the steady state of full linguistic competence that every human being reaches is so rich, complex and particular that it can only be explained by hypothesising a highly structured and specific initial state of linguistic ability. We cannot directly observe or study the initial state but, Chomsky claims, we are justified in proposing it as the best working solution to the logical problem of language acquisition. Imitation alone cannot explain language acquisition because there is not sufficient good-quality data to imitate.

9.4   Child-directed speech

For every theory about language there are of course linguists who will disagree with it. Chomsky's IH is no exception to this rule. As might be expected, many objections to it have been based on the premise that Chomsky's 'mentalist' approach to language is wrong-headed and that linguists should be analysing not a complex internal structure of the mind, but the process by which children learn the ability to communicate with those around them. We will consider one such alternative approach in the next section.

Other linguists have taken issue with the more specific claims about language and people that Chomsky has used to justify the innateness hypothesis. For instance it has been argued that children's ability to learn language is not actually as remarkable as Chomsky has made out, if you consider that for the first few years of their lives there a few demands on their time other than learning language. You can find references to objections of this type in the 'Further reading' section at the end of this chapter.

One particular line of research in the area of language acquisition has focused on Chomsky's claim about the 'poverty of stimulus': the idea that the evidence for the language that the child receives is so poor and incomplete that it cannot explain successful acquisition. Chomsky's insistence that everyday language use is full of errors and omissions seems plausible enough. However in the 1970s a number of linguists challenged the assumption that observations about everyday language could necessarily be used in discussions of the input to the process of acquisition. In an article published in 1986, Catherine Snow introduced this topic by pointing out that 'Only ten or fifteen years ago it was thought possible to study language acquisition without studying the language addressed to children' (Snow, 1986, p. 69). Claims had been made about the language children heard as input, and weighty theoretical conclusions had been based on these claims. But there had been no attempt to establish by observation whether the claims were justified.

Researchers in this area argued that the language addressed to young children was just not the same as other types of everyday language. They investigated this type of language by experiment and observation, and at first referred to it as 'mothers' speech'. When it was realised that the type of language in question was used not just by mothers but also by other adults, and indeed even by older children, this term was later changed to 'child-directed speech' (CDS). Researchers such as Catherine Snow and others argued that CDS had certain distinctive characteristics that set it apart as a specific variety of English.

The distinctive characterisics of CDS make up a quite complex and diverse list (these are discussed in detail in some of the works listed in the 'Further reading' section at the end of this chapter). The utterances produced when addressing young children are said to be generally shorter than those produced when addressing other adults. They are also simpler grammatically, avoiding complicated structures such as subordinate clauses and passives. They tend to be more correct and more fluent; utterances in CDS generally do not contain many grammatical errors, false starts or hesitations. They are characterised by a high degree of redundancy; that is, they include a lot of words that are not strictly necessary because they repeat either exactly or roughly what has already been said. In terms of content and subject matter, CDS tends to focus on the here and now: on what is immediately present in the context of the conversation. Overall CDS is said to be characterised by 'fine tuning'. Speech addressed to a young child does not stay the same but changes gradually over time. It becomes more complex as the child becomes older; it might be said to be 'tuned' to the child's ability to understand and respond.

From the point of view of alternative theories of language, the most interesting part of the work on CDS is how Snow and others responded to these characteristics: the conclusions they drew from them. In fact they were surprisingly modest in their claims. For instance Snow did not argue that her research indicated that Chomsky must be completely wrong, or that it proved that language was not innate. She actually agreed with Chomsky that there was no evidence that children were directly taught language as they were taught other skills. Adults' motivation in using CDS was to interact and communicate with children, not to teach them. However Snow argued that it was at least possible that the features of CDS offered young children a very useful model for building up a picture of the language they were learning, and that therefore some of Chomsky's more extreme claims should be treated with caution. The input that children received in fact looked remarkably like an effective set of 'language lessons' (Snow, 1972, p. 561).

By placing this phrase in quotation marks, Snow was obviously keen to distance herself from the suggestion that adults deliberately taught language to children in this way. Language that was simple, short and redundant offered children numerous examples of basic syntactic structures. Meanwhile language that was concerned with the here and now helped children to develop an understanding of meaning, and of the relationship between individual words and objects. In both respects the language the child was exposed to gradually become more complex over time, meaning that the child was constantly encouraged to develop further syntactic and semantic ability.

CDS research certainly did not cause Chomsky's innateness hypothesis to be abandoned. It did, however, suggest another way of looking at things, and drew attention to some unsupported assumptions about input in Chomsky's work. There are problems, however, for anyone who wants to claim that CDS is sufficient to explain away the logical problem of language acquisition. Perhaps most significantly, there is evidence that CDS is far from universal. Some of the early claims about its importance may have been based on the assumption that what went on in particular types of family – specifically middle-class, academic, American families – went on everywhere. But there is evidence that in some cultures there simply is no such thing as CDS. Children are either not addressed at all, or addressed only with commands and explanations. Nevertheless, as Chomsky himself has noted, children learn a first language with similar speed and success whatever culture they grow up in. It is certainly possible that CDS has a role to play in language learning, but it seems that it cannot be an essential role. One of Snow's modest arguments was that studying CDS 'makes it somewhat easier to understand how a child can accomplish the formidable task of learning his native language with such relative ease' (ibid., p. 564).

9.5　Functional learning

As we have seen, Snow was adamant that whatever its effects on language learning the motivation behind using CDS was to communicate with children. For her the concentration on the child's mental development that was fundamental to the innateness hypothesis was artificial. It meant that theorists working in the Chomskyan tradition were attempting to explain language acquisition without reference to the social and communicative environment in which it occurred. In one of her articles, she set out some basic assumptions about language acquisition that she claimed had become widely accepted, at least in part as a result of CDS research. Her list began with the following assumption:

> Language acquisition is the result of a process of interaction between mother and child which begins early in infancy, to which the child makes as important a contribution as the mother, and which is crucial to cognitive and emotional development as well as to language acquisition (Snow, 1977, pp. 31–2).

In this one sentence Snow identified many of the significant features of an alternative to Chomsky's account of language acquisition that developed during the 1970s. This came to be known as the functional approach to language acquisition. This approach was based on a functional view of language more generally: that is, on a view of language as being defined and shaped by the different functions it was used to perform in communication in a particular society.

This approach to language acquisition took Halliday's (1975) functional account of language as its starting point. We considered Halliday's work in Part I as an example of a set of ideas based on the belief that language is communication. We saw there that Halliday's interests are applied as well as theoretical. In particular, he has been interested in analysing children's language in relation to language learning. He argued that the innateness hypothesis had led to an almost exclusive interest in syntax and structure in discussions of language learning. The problem with this was that it forced linguists to ignore what for Halliday were the most important aspects of language: that it was meaningful, that it occurred in particular contexts, and that it was used for communication. For Halliday an account of language that ignored these features was just missing the point. As Halliday himself put it, those studying language acquisition should replace the question 'How does the child acquire structure?' with the question 'How does the child learn language?', on the understanding that language involved much more than just structure (Halliday, 1975, pp. 1–3). Indeed for Halliday learning a language involved more than all the formal properties that together made up a grammar, including vocabulary and phonology. It also involved learning to use the language appropriately to communicate in different contexts. A satisfactory account of language in general, and of language acquisition in particular, would only be possible once the situational, communicative and interactive aspects of language were taken in to account.

A further consequence of the concentration on syntax and structure, and for Halliday a further weakness of this concentration, was that discussions of language acquisition tended to start only once there was some evidence of syntactic awareness: that is, once children started putting words together to form simple two-word utterances. Linguists were interested in this stage because it provided evidence of the emergence of grammar, in the awareness that children displayed that word order was significant. Halliday argued that a study that started at this stage of development would already have missed a lot of important evidence because it would have missed the beginnings of the child's understanding of communication. In contrast, 'From a functional point of view, as soon as there are meaningful expressions there is language, and the investigation can begin at a time before words and structures have evolved to take over the burden of realisation' (ibid., p. 6).

Functional linguists therefore looked to the very earliest vocalisations for evidence of the intention to communicate. Some functional linguists, such as John Dore (1974) argued that cries could be interpreted as what he called 'primitive speech acts' such as requests. Halliday himself began his record of language learning when the ten-month-old infant he was studying was starting to show evidence of the intention to communicate. Although there was no grammar at this stage, Halliday identified functions such as the 'instrumental', the 'regulatory', the 'interactional' and the 'personal' in the baby's vocal output (Halliday, 1975, p. 39). The child's utterances of single words or even single syllables at later stages were given 'translations' into the adult system. For instance the child's *Nò* in response to *do you want some cheese?* was interpreted as *No I don't want it.* The sound *à* in response to *Shall I put the lorry in the box for you?* was interpreted as *Yes do* (ibid., p. 46).

It would be unfair to criticise Halliday for reading too much into the child's words just because the child did not have a grasp of the adult linguistic system. His point was that, despite this, the child was capable of some quite complex communicative intentions: intentions that could be paraphrased in the adult linguistic system in the ways he suggested. The child's linguistic abilities would eventually catch up with his or her communicative intentions, and indeed this process would be driven at least in part by the desire to communicate those intentions. In this way the child would proceed through a series of stages towards the adult cognitive and linguistic level of development.

Another linguist working within the functional framework, Elizabeth Bates (1976), concentrated on the development of aspects of language use that were traditionally considered to be pragmatic. She argued that the innateness hypothesis had ruled out considerations of social function in the process of language acquisition. Looking at abilities in areas such as speech acts, presupposition and conversational implicature was one way of shifting the focus towards the social. Like Halliday, she contrasted the type of question asked by Chomsky in his studies of language acquisition with the type of question she thought was more appropriate. Chomsky was concerned with how a child learnt structure. Bates was more concerned with the more pragmatic question of why a child learnt to talk at all: 'A study of the acquisition of performatives is, basically, a study of how children arrive at the intention to communicate' (Bates, 1976, p. 49).

For functional linguists, language was not a separate mental capacity but part of a child's general mental development. Linguistic ability emerged as the child became aware of the need to communicate progressively more complex messages. As Snow explained in the passage quoted at the start of this section, linguistic development and more general cognitive development were inextricably linked. A further consequence of this was that it made little sense to study linguistic ability and the ability to use language for certain purposes as separate capacities. There was no point trying to separate the study of grammar from the study of pragmatics, because grammar came into play only when people wanted to do certain things with language: when they wanted to affect other people in certain ways.

9.6　Further reading

See Clark (2006, ch. 1) for a discussion of language varieties and practical advice on how to research variation in English. There is no direct discussion of CDS, but the ideas and techniques covered are relevant to any empirical investigation of conversations between adults and children, and to the claim that CDS is a separate variety of English.

The discussion of language learning in terms of imitation in this chapter has focused mainly on the overtly behaviourist account in Skinner (1957). But as mentioned, this is not the only way in which language learning has been explained in terms of imitation. Quine's description of the child as being like a traveller in a foreign country can be found in Quine (1960). Quine's ideas on this topic are discussed in Martin (1987, ch. 6) and are compared with Chomsky's innateness hypothesis in Chapman (2000, ch. 5) and Stainton (1996, ch. 8). Language learning is also described in terms of imitation in Bloomfield (1935).

As discussed, Chomsky developed the implications of the innateness hypothesis for language acquisition in a large number of books (see for example Chomsky, 1966, 1980, 1986). His 1987 book also deals with these issues and is aimed at non-specialists. The implications for theories of language acquisition for viewing language as a complex, structured type of knowledge are discussed in Goodluck (1986). Critics of Chomsky included

Hilary Putnam (1967) who challenged the necessity of the hypothesis to explain language acquisition, and Nelson Goodman (1984), who questioned the uniformity of human languages.

The literature on CDS, mainly dating from the 1970s, is extensive. Snow and Ferguson (1977) contains a useful collection of essays on the subject, and Snow (1977) provides a good overview of the field. Similarly there is a great deal of literature on language learning from a functional perspective. Here we have considered briefly the book-length studies by Halliday (1975) and Bates (1976). John Dore wrote a number of articles on primitive speech acts (see for example Dore, 1974, 1975). Interesting collections of essays in this field are Ochs and Schieffelin (1979) and Wanner and Gleitman (1982).

A Final Thought: Do Other Animals Have Language?

Throughout history, human beings have found it necessary or desirable to communicate with other animals. There is no doubt that to some extent exchange of meaning between humans and animals is possible. Some people may have exaggerated ideas about pets who 'understand everything that's said to them', but it is clear that horses and dogs, for instance, can be trained to obey a range of spoken commands. In return guide dogs and sheep dogs can convey simple messages to their handlers by sounds or behaviour. The ability to communicate is certainly not limited to human beings, but this is of course not necessarily the same thing as the ability to use language.

The differences between theories of language are particularly significant when we approach the question of whether other animals have language. Perhaps more than for any of the other questions we have considered in this section, the answer has to begin with 'It depends what you mean by language . . . ' If language were no more than a basic ability to communicate, then we would have to reply with a simple and rather uninformative 'Yes'. But of course defining language in this way would raise more problems than it solves. For instance the examples of animal communication we have just considered allow for the transmission of only a very limited range of messages compared with what we can do with human language. The philosopher Bertrand Russell, whose debate with Strawson about definite descriptions we considered in Chapter 8, commented that 'A dog cannot relate his autobiography; however eloquently he may bark, he cannot tell you that his parents were honest though poor' (Russell, 1948, p. 133).

Attempts to decide whether language is unique to humans have tended to take one of two paths. Researchers have concentrated either on establishing whether other animals have complex communication systems that we should call languages, or on investigating whether particular animals can be taught to use and understand some form of human language. We will briefly consider some of these attempts in this chapter. The results of these studies have varied considerably, and so too have the ways in which researchers have interpreted their results. Decisions about whether the studies indicate that non-humans have language, or at least a capacity for language, will always be based on a previous set of decisions. These are decisions about the question with which we started: What is language?

The different ways of answering this question that we have been concerned with in this book go a long way towards explaining why researchers confronted with the same evidence can have widely different views on whether other animals have language. For instance it is no surprise to find that mentalist linguists, working in the Chomskyan tradition, argue very definitely that language is unique to humans. For them, language is part of the genetic and biological make-up of human beings. Other animals may be capable of being trained to mimic human behaviour in some respects, but this does not mean that they can acquire human language. The only way to do this is to have a human mind.

For those who see language as a type of behaviour the picture is completely different. If humans learn language through a complex process of conditioning, and if this process is essentially the same as that which determines animal behaviour, there is in principle no reason why animals could not learn human language. The possible limitations in this case will not be genetic but to do with animals' capacity for learning, and perhaps with the practicality of the time such a process might take. Not all theorists who reject mentalism are behaviourists, of course. For those who define language as fundamentally a system of communication there is no reason in theory why animals, or certain types of animal, might not be said to have language. But such theorists are faced with the question of the intention to convey information that is normally said to accompany communication, and of whether we can be certain that animals have that intention as well as displaying the appropriate behaviour.

Discussions of the relationship between language and other, non-human forms of communication sometimes include the terms 'continuity' and 'discontinuity'. These terms provide a useful way of thinking abut some of the main issues. Those who argue that language is continuous with other forms of communication are saying that there is no essential difference that sets language apart. It might be much more complex than any of the animal communication systems that scientists have identified, but it is basically the same type of thing. Continuity theorists generally argue that human language has simply developed over time out of more primitive communication systems that are similar to those still found among animals. Discontinuity theorists, on the other hand, argue that language is fundamentally different from any other form of communication. Rather than placing language on a scale of communication systems of varying complexity, they see it as a totally separate type of entity, unique in the natural world. It is not possible to explain it as simply developing gradually from more primitive systems; it exists as an essential and unique feature of the evolved human brain. Needless to say, Chomskyan linguists explain language in terms of discontinuity.

One general feature of studies of the naturally occurring communication systems of animals is the finding that they show far more complexity than simple series of cries relating to territory, food or mating. Just two examples, which are often cited in discussions of animals and language, are communication among bees and among vervet monkeys. Studies of bees undertaken in the 1950s revealed that they communicate with each other using a series of bodily movements, or a 'dance'. Researchers noted that a bee that had just returned to the hive would be surrounded by other bees, and by orientating its body in a particular manner and moving at a particular rate it appeared to pass on information about the direction and distance of a food source. After observing this dance the other bees consistently flew directly to the food source.

Observations of vervet monkeys concentrated on vocalisation. Thomas Struhsaker (1967) observed that the monkeys' repertoire of cries was prompted by what he described as different 'stimulus situations'. In particular they had a number of different cries that relate to different types of danger. As with the bee dance, the success of this system of communication was judged in terms of the animals responding to the cries. They reacted in consistently particular ways to the different vocalisations. For instance on hearing the cry generally produced by a monkey who had seen an eagle, the other monkeys would move from trees or open grassland to hide in dense thickets. On hearing the cry associated with a predator such as a big cat, the vervets ran into the trees.

Studies such as these suggest that animals have developed systems for communicating some quite complex messages. It might seem only fair to allow that animals, or at least some animals, do actually have languages of their own. These may differ in many respects from human languages, but this may not be a legitimate reason for disqualifying them. Perhaps the most persuasive argument against this conclusion relates to the notion of creativity in language. This is one implication of Bertrand Russell's observation that a dog cannot tell us its autobiography. As we have seen, one of the features of human language is that it is possible to produce entirely new sentences, to describe new experiences, and be confident that they will be understood by someone who speaks the same language. It is far from clear, however, that there are any animal communication systems that share this property. Bees and vervet monkeys may be able to convey a complex range of messages, but these messages are finite. A bee could not communicate by means of a dance its hope that it will find a better source of food tomorrow. A vervet monkey could not tell the other monkeys about its memories of a particularly scary jaguar attack last year.

Some experimental support for this claim comes from the original bee studies. When a bee found food that had been placed on top of a high pole it was unable to tell the other bees about it on returning to the hive. It had no way of explaining this new circumstance in a dance, and the other bees were unable to locate the food source. This evidence is of course not conclusive; it does not prove that bees or vervet monkeys do not have language. However it does draw attention to the fact that if we want to say that creativity is an essential feature of language, then we cannot really define the communication systems of these animals as languages. Whether we decide that creativity is in fact essential or that it is simply claimed by human beings to be essential because it is a feature of their communication systems, depends as always on our views on what language is.

Research that involves trying to teach some form of human language to animals might have a good chance of avoiding the problem of creativity. If an animal can be taught adequately to use something that is already recognised as a language, it would surely be reasonable to claim that the animal is linguistically capable. Even if animals have not naturally developed anything as complex in their own communication systems, this might indicate that they nevertheless have the capacity to do so. It would suggest that human beings are not in fact unique in their language ability. This would not necessarily rule out the possibility that language is innate, but we would at least have to allow that it was an innate ability that is shared by some non-human animals. Some researchers have expressed another hope for these studies. If animals can be taught language, they might be able to describe their experiences to us: to tell us what it is like to be a non-human.

Perhaps not surprisingly, attempts to teach language to animals have generally concentrated on those which are genetically closest to humans: the great apes, and particularly chimpanzees. This choice has not necessarily been motivated by a belief in a genetically shared language faculty. But it has certainly drawn on the assumption that chimpanzees' relatively high intelligence and physical similarity to humans offer the best possible chance of success. The earliest scientifically documented attempt, dating from the 1930s, involved bringing up an infant chimpanzee in a human family environment. The plan was to investigate whether chimpanzees, like human beings, were capable of acquiring language if they were constantly exposed to it as they grew up. The first attempt was a complete failure in that the chimpanzee never produced any spoken utterances. A later attempt in the 1950s fared little better. In this case the animal learnt only a handful of words, and even these were articulated indistinctly and with great difficulty.

The main conclusion drawn from these experiments was that it was an unfair test for chimpanzees. Despite the obvious physical similarities, chimpanzees were physiologically very different from humans. Particularly significantly, because their larynxes and mouths had a different structure they simply could not articulate human speech sounds. So the failure of the attempts did not indicate that chimpanzees did not have the mental capacity to master language, only that they did not have the physical capacity to produce speech. Later attempts therefore concentrated on forms of language that might be better suited to an ape's physical abilities.

American sign language (ASL) proved particularly popular with researchers. As we saw in Chapter 6, ASL is a complex, structured and creative human language. It was used in work by Beatrice and Allen Gardner (1971), who reared an infant chimpanzee in a specially created 'house' in a laboratory. The Gardners and the other researchers working with them used ASL to communicate about everyday events with Washoe, as they called the chimpanzee. They were impressed by the number of signs that Washoe apparently learnt to recognise and to use appropriately, although they remained deliberately non-committal about whether she might be said to have acquired language. In fact they pointed out that deciding on this question was dependent on the definition of language:

> There are ways to define language that would permit us to say that Washoe achieved language . . . There are other ways to define language, and undoubtedly the term could be defined in such a way that no chimpanzee could ever achieve language (Gardner and Gardner, 1971, p. 181).

As they were psychologists rather than linguists, the Gardners were more interested in the possibilities of animal communication than the technicalities of language. Nevertheless they did make some assumptions about language that necessarily affected their approach to the project and the degree to which they were impressed by its success. It is clear that for the Gardners language was best defined and studied as a type of behaviour. As they themselves noted: 'This assumption leads directly to the hypothesis that behavior that is at least continuous with human language can be found in other species' (ibid., p. 118). In other words, if language was no different in type but perhaps just in complexity from other forms of behaviour, there was no reason why chimpanzees could not display at least a limited grasp of language. The alternative point of view, not discussed by the Gardners, is of course to see language as a particular mental capacity or set of knowledge. Based on this assumption it might be argued that all types of animal communication, including Washoe's attempts at ASL, are *dis*continuous with language; they are a different type of thing altogether. With this view it is not nearly as straightforward to allow that a chimpanzee can display a limited grasp of language. Linguistic ability is something you either have or do not have. It is therefore necessary to think much more precisely about what are the essential features of linguistic ability.

This issue was confronted by Herbert Terrace (1980), another researcher who attempted to teach ASL to a chimpanzee. Terrace named the chimpanzee Nim Chimpsky, in a reflection of his scepticism about the theories of Noam Chomsky. Nim was not brought up in a normal human environment but was attended throughout the day by people drawn from a fairly large group of trainers. The task of the trainers was to attempt to communicate with Nim using ASL, and to record any signs that he produced. Terrace was initially very impressed by the number of signs that Nim learnt and used correctly during the course of the project, and he was confident that this would strengthen the case for arguing that language was not unique to humans. However when the project was over and he looked in more detail at the written records and videotapes that had been collected, he began to revise his opinion.

Terrace noticed that, unlike what would be expected from a developing child, the average length of Nim's utterances, in terms of the number of different signs used, did not advance beyond 1.6. Some of Nim's utterances were much longer than this, but what at first had appeared to be impressively long sequences of signs turned out to be made up mainly of repetition. Nim's longest utterance was *Give orange me give eat orange me eat orange give me eat orange give me you*. While this utterance was long it did not contain any more information than a very short utterance would have done. Certainly it did not appear to reflect any of the syntactic rules that governed fully structured human languages. Terrace began to suspect that the same could be said of the much shorter utterances. When Nim used combinations of three signs these did not generally add any more information than similar combinations of two signs. Moreover there did not appear to be any grammatical rules to explain the addition of an extra sign. The trainers had recorded both *play me* and *play me Nim*; *eat Nim* and *Nim eat Nim*; *sweet Nim* and *sweet Nim sweet*.

A further problem that confronted Terrace when he watched the videotapes of the project was that Nim mainly used signs that he had just observed the trainers using. Only 10 per cent of Nim's utterance were spontaneous in that they were not produced in response to signing from a trainer. In contrast about 40 per cent were either imitations or shortened versions of the immediately preceding utterances of the trainers. Nim's utterances were much less spontaneous and much more imitative than would be expected from a young child. Terrace was forced to admit that he had not in fact collected evidence that a chimpanzee had learnt language. Here is his reluctant conclusion:

It would be premature to conclude that a chimpanzee's combinations show the same structure evident in the sentences of a child. The fact that Nim's utterances were less spontaneous and less original than those of a child and that his utterances did not become longer, both as he learned new signs and as he acquired more experience in using sign language, suggests that much of the structure and meaning of his combinations was determined, or at least suggested, by the utterances of his teachers (Terrace, 1980, p. 221).

All he had was evidence that Nim was intelligent enough to imitate his trainers in order to get what he wanted. Terrace did not, however, go as far as completely changing his position and conceding that Chomsky must have been right all along. He remained convinced that it might yet be possible to teach ASL to a chimpanzee, given a better set of circumstances. If sufficient funds were made available to keep a project going for longer than the Nim project had been able to do, and if a smaller number of trainers could be employed to provide a stable environment and extensive teaching, it might one day be possible for a chimpanzee to learn ASL. However Terrace's insistence on the need for careful and extensive training to achieve this goal itself makes an interesting contrast with the human situation, if you subscribe to the view that children acquire language easily and without teaching.

Rather more confident claims have been made about another great ape who was the subject in a language research project: Kanzi, a bonobo, or pygmy chimpanzee. Sue Savage-Rumbaugh is convinced that Kanzi provides evidence that great apes can learn language, and hence that their minds are not necessarily as different from human minds as has sometimes been assumed or claimed (see for example Savage-Rumbaugh and Lewin, 1994). What is striking about Kanzi is that, at least initially, the development of his ability to communicate was not the result of any explicit teaching. Savage-Rumbaugh and her fellow researchers chose to use a keyboard of 'lexigrams' in their work with bonobos. This was a computerised board on which a series of keys were labelled with symbols. Each symbol had arbitrarily been assigned a meaning, and the researchers pressed the relevant keys as they interacted with the bonobos. They had been trying to teach Kanzi's mother to communicate using the lexigrams, but without a great deal of success. However they discovered almost by accident that Kanzi, who had been observing these attempts but had not been directly involved in them, had developed an understanding of the use of the keyboard and of the meaning of some of the symbols, and moreover was eager to start using them. The researchers claimed that Kanzi had also developed an understanding of a range of spoken English words, just by hearing them.

Savage-Rumbaugh was impressed by the range and accuracy of the vocabulary of lexigrams that Kanzi developed, and by his ability to combine these to produce longer utterances. In fact, however, the transcriptions of these utterances appear no more impressive than Nim Chimpsky's output. But Savage-Rumbaugh responded differently from Terrace to the results of her project because she takes a different approach to the question of what is essential to language. For her, the insistence that language must be syntactically structured is an unnecessary imposition by linguists. She is dismissive of what she calls the 'extraordinary emphasis on syntax as the *sine qua non* of language' (Savage-Rumbaugh and Lewin, 1994, p. 125); that is, the insistence by linguists that without syntax there is no language. Once you dispense with what she sees as this unjustified obsession with syntax, it is possible to describe Kanzi as having exhibited linguistic ability. This view is, as Savage-Rumbaugh acknowledges, based on a 'continuity' of communication that sees nothing special about human language. Discussion of partial linguistic ability is therefore legitimate: 'As the ape-brain is just one-third the size of the human brain, we should accept the detection of no more than a few elements of language as evidence of continuity' (ibid., p. 164). Yet again, judgments of whether Kanzi's case supports the claim that some animals are capable of language depend on views of the nature of language. Those who maintain that syntactic structure is essential to language will obviously look at the evidence from Kanzi and see no more than an intelligent and socialised ape.

Chomsky himself has been predictably unimpressed by the results of attempts to teach language to apes: 'The interesting investigations of the capacity of the higher apes to acquire symbolic systems seem to me to support the traditional belief that even the most rudimentary properties of language lie well beyond the capacities of an otherwise intelligent ape' (Chomsky, 1980, p. 239). He comments on the extreme unlikelihood of finding anything like the human language faculty in any other species. There is no evidence of anything approaching a complex, structured language occurring naturally other than in human beings. It is therefore odd to hope to prove that some animals are nevertheless capable of language; to argue, in effect, that apes have the ability to use language but have never got round to doing so.

One other aspect of the studies with apes that has proved controversial, and shows every sign of remaining so, is the extent to which the animals in question can be said to have displayed consciousness of the process of communication. It is very hard to provide evidence that apes are using language to describe the world around them in the same way that humans do, in other words that they are self-aware enough to form an intention to communicate, rather than simply responding cleverly and subtly to clues from their trainers. This is one problem that casts some doubt on the possibility of ever being able fully to communicate with animals in the way that some researchers have hoped: to find out what it is like to be a chimpanzee, for instance.

Another problem with this idea is that even if an ape could learn a human language it might not be able to express its own experiences. It would be trying to express ape experiences in a human language, a language necessarily developed from humans' understanding and perception of the world. Ludwig Wittgenstein, the philosopher often credited with the idea that 'meaning is use', once wrote that 'if a lion could talk, we could not understand him' (Wittgenstein, quoted in Kenny, 1994, p. 213). A lion's way of life is very different from a human way of life. It has different ways of perceiving and understanding the world, and finds different experiences significant. If a lion did have language it would want to do very different things with it than humans do. To use Wittgenstein's own metaphor, it would want to play different language games. So even if we could miraculously teach a human language to a lion, it is highly probable that we and the lion would not be able to make any sense of what we were saying to each other.

Further reading

The original work on the communicative dance of bees is presented in Von Frisch (1950). Further discussion of this, together with a report on bees' inability to describe novel situations, can be found in Von Frisch (1954). A report on the research into the vocalisations of vervet monkeys is contained in Struhsaker (1967).

The literature on attempts to teach various forms of human language to apes is vast. With regard to the projects described in this chapter, the first attempt to teach a chimpanzee language by bringing it up in a human family, and the failure of this attempt, is documented in Kellog and Kellog (1933). The later, only slightly more successful attempt is described in Hayes (1951). Both experiments are also discussed in Brown (1958). The Gardners have written extensively about their work with Washoe. A useful single article is Gardner and Gardner (1971), but see also their 1969 and 1984 works. The project with Nim Chimpsky, and the rather disappointing conclusions drawn from it, are discussed in Terrace (1980). Sue Savage-Rumbaugh reported on her work with Kanzi in a number of articles, including Greenfield and Savage-Rumbaugh (1990). She later coauthoured a book with Roger Lewin (1994) about Kanzi and what she saw as the implications of his success in learning language. An overview of all these research projects with apes can be found in Aitchison (1998).

Bibliography

Aitchison, Jean (1998) *The Articulate Mammal*, 4th edn (London: Routledge).

Allwood, Jens, Lars Gunnar Andersson and Osten Dahl (1979) *Logic in Linguistics* (Cambridge: Cambridge University Press).

Austin, J. L. (1956) 'A plea for excuses', *Proceedings of the Aristotelian Society*, reprinted in J. L. Austin (1961) *Philosophical Papers* (Oxford: Clarendon Press), pp. 123–52.

Austin, J. L. (1962) *How to do Things with Words* (Oxford: Oxford University Press).

Avramides, Anita (1989) *Meaning and Mind* (Cambridge, Mass.: MIT Press).

Ayer, A. J. (1971) *Language Truth and Logic* (Harmondsworth: Pelican).

Ayer, A. J. (1976) *The Central Questions of Philosophy* (Harmondsworth: Pelican).

Bach, Kent (2001) 'You don't say?', *Synthesis*, vol. 128, pp. 15–44.

Barthes, Roland (1968) *Elements of Semiology*, trans. Annette Lavers and Colin Smith (New York: Hill & Wang).

Bates, Elizabeth (1976) *Language and Context* (New York: Academic Press).

Blakemore, Diane (1994) *Understanding Utterances* (Oxford: Blackwell).

Bloomfield, Leonard (1935) *Language* (London: Allen & Unwin).

Brown, E. R. (1958) *Words and Things* (New York: Free Press).

Brown, Penelope and Stephen Levinson (1987) *Politeness* (Cambridge: Cambridge University Press).

Carnap, Rudolf (1937) *The Logical Syntax of Language* (London: Routledge & Keegan Paul).

Chapman, Siobhan (2000) *Philosophy for Linguists* (London: Routledge).

Chapman, Siobhan (2005) *Paul Grice, Philosopher and Linguist* (Basingstoke: Palgrave Macmillan).

Chomsky, Noam (1957) *Syntactic Structures* (The Hague: Mouton).

Chomsky, Noam (1959) 'Review of *Verbal Behavior* by B. F. Skinner', *Language*, vol. 35, pp. 26–58).

Chomsky, Noam (1965) *Aspects of the Theory of Syntax* (Cambridge, Mass.: MIT Press).

Chomsky, Noam (1966) *Cartesian Linguistics* (New York: Harper & Row).

Chomsky, Noam (1968) 'Recent contributions to the theory of innate ideas', *Boston Studies in the Philosophy of Science*, vol. 3, reprinted in J. R. Searle, *The Philosophy of Language* (Oxford: Oxford University Press, 1971), pp. 121–9.

Chomsky, Noam (1969) 'Quine's empirical assunptions', in Donald Davidson and Jaakko Hintikka (eds), *Words and Objections* (Dordrecht: D. Reidel), pp. 53–68.

Chomsky, Noam (1971) 'Topics in the Theory of Generative Grammar', in J. R. Searle (ed.), *The Philosophy of Language* (Oxford: Oxford University Press), pp. 71–100.

Chomsky, Noam (1980) *Rules and Representations* (Oxford: Blackwell).

Chomsky, Noam (1981) *Lectures on Government and Binding* (Dordrecht: Foris).

Chomsky, Noam (1986) *Knowledge of Language* (New York: Praeger).

Chomsky, Noam (1987) *Language and the Problems of Knowledge* (Cambridge, Mass.: MIT Press).

Chomsky, Noam (1995) *The Minimalist Program* (Cambridge, Mass.: MIT Press).

Clark, Urszula (2006) *Studying Language: English in Action* (Basingstoke: Palgrave).

Clarke, D. S. Jnr (1987) *Principles of Semiotic* (London: Routledge & Kegan Paul).

Cole, Peter (ed.) (1981) *Radical Pragmatics* (New York: Academic Press).

Davidson, Donald (1967) 'Truth and meaning', *Synthese*, vol. 17, pp. 304–23.

Davidson, Donald (1979) 'Moods and Performatives', in Avishai Margalit (ed.), *Meaning and Use* (Dordrecht: Reidel), pp. 9–20.

Devitt, Michael and Kim Sterelny (1987) *Language and Reality* (Oxford: Blackwell).

Dore, John (1974) 'A pragmatic description of early language development', *Journal of Psycholinguistic Research*, vol. 3, pp. 343–50.

Dore, John (1975) 'Holophrases, speech acts and language universals', *Journal of Child Language*, vol. 2, pp. 21–40.

Evnine, Simon (1991) *Donald Davidson* (Cambridge: Polity Press).

Fairclough, Norman (1989) *Language and Power* (Harlow: Longman).

Firth, J. R. (1957) *Papers in Linguistics* (London: Oxford University Press).

Fodor, Jerry (1976) *The Language of Thought* (Hassocks: Harvester Press).

Frege, Gottlob (1980) 'On sense and meaning', in Peter Geach and Max Black (eds), *Translations from the Philosophical Writings of Gottlob Frege* (Oxford: Blackwell).

Gardner, Beatrice T. and R. Allen Gardner (1971) 'Two-way communication with an infant chimpanzee', in Allan M. Schrier and Fred Stollnitz (eds), *Behavior of Non-human Primates*, vol. 4 (New York: Academic Press), pp. 117–84.

Gardner, R. Allen and Beatrice T. Gardner (1969) 'Teaching sign language to a chimpanzee', *Science*, vol. 165, pp. 664–72.

Gardner, R. Allen and Beatrice T. Gardner (1984) 'A vocabulary test for chimpanzees (Pan troglodytes)', *Journal of Comparative Psychology*, vol. 96, pp. 381–404.

Gazdar, Gerald (1979) *Pragmatics* (New York: Academic Press).

Gibbon, Margaret (1999) *Feminist Perspectives on Language* (London: Longman).

Goodluck, Helen (1986) 'Language acquisition and linguistic theory', in Paul Fletcher and Michael Garman (eds), *Language Acquisition*, 2nd edn (Cambridge: Cambridge University Press) pp. 49–68.

Goodman, Nelson (1984) *Of Mind and Other Matters* (Cambridge, Mass.: Harvard University Press).

Greenfield, Patricia Marks and Sue Savage-Rumbaugh (1990) 'Grammatical combinations in *pan paniscus*: processes of learning and invention in the evolution and development of language', in Sue T. Parker and Kathleen Gibson, *'Language' and Intelligence in Monkeys and Apes: Comparative Developmental Perspectives* (Cambridge: Cambridge University Press).

Grice, Paul (1957) 'Meaning', *The Philosophical Review*, vol. 66, reprinted in Paul Grice, *Studies in the Way of Words* (Cambridge, Mass.: Harvard University Press, 1989) pp. 213–23.

Grice, Paul (1975) Logic and conversation', in P. Cole and J. Morgan (eds), *Syntax and Semantics, volume 3* (New York: Academic Press), reprinted in Paul Grice *Studies in the Way of Words* (Cambridge, Mass.: Harvard University Press, 1989) pp. 22–40.

Grice, Paul (1981) 'Presupposition and conversational implicature', in Peter Cole (ed.), *Radical Pragmatics* (New York: Academic Press), reprinted in Paul Grice, *Studies in the Way of Words* (Cambridge, Mass.: Harvard University Press, 1989), pp. 269–82.

Grice, Paul (1989) *Studies in the Way of Words* (Cambridge, Mass.: Harvard University Press).

Grice, Paul and Peter Strawson (1956) 'In defence of a dogma', *The Philosophical Review*, vol. 65, pp. 141–58, reprinted in Paul Grice, *Studies in the Way of Words* (Cambridge, Mass.: Harvard University Press, 1989), pp. 304–38.

Halliday, M. A. K. (1975) *Learning how to Mean* (London: Edward Arnold).

Halliday, M. A. K. (1985) *An Introduction to Functional Grammar* (London: Edward Arnold).

Harris, Roy (1996) *Signs, Language and Communication* (London: Routledge).

Harris, Roy (1998) 'Language as social interaction: integrationalism versus segregationalism', in Roy Harris and George Wolf, *Integrational Linguistics* (Amsterdam: Pergamon Press), pp. 5–14.

Hawkes, Terrence (1977) *Structuralism and Semiotics* (London: Methuen).

Hayes, C. (1951) *The Ape in Our House* (New York: Harper).

Honey, John (1997) *Language is Power* (London: Faber & Faber).

Horn, Larry (1989) *A Natural History of Negation* (Chicago, Ill.: University of Chicago Press).

Hymes, Dell (1974) *Foundations in Sociolinguistics* (Philadelphia, PA: University of Pennsylvania Press).

Jeffries, Lesley (2006) *Discovering Language: The Structure of Modern English* (Basingstoke: Palgrave).

Johnstone, Barbara (2002) *Discourse Analysis* (Oxford: Blackwell).

Kant, Immanuel (1929) *Critique of Pure Reason*, trans. Norman Kemp Smith (London: Macmillan).

Kellog, W. N. and L. A. Kellog (1933) *The Ape and the Child* (New York: McGraw-Hill).

Kennedy, Graeme (1998) *An Introduction to Corpus Linguistics* (London: Addison Wesley Longman).

Kenny, Anthony (1994) *The Wittgenstein Reader* (Oxford: Blackwell).

Kristeva, Julia (1989) *Language: The Unknown: An Initiation into Linguistics*, trans. Anne M. Menke (London, Sydney and Toronto: Harvester Wheatsheaf).

Labov, William (1972) 'Some principles of linguistic methodology', *Language in Society*, vol. 1, pp. 97–120.

Lakoff, George and Mark Johnson (1980) *Metaphors We Live By* (Chicago, Ill.: University of Chicago Press).

Leech, Geoffrey (1983) *Principles of Pragmatics* (Harlow: Longman).

Levinson, Stephen. (1983) *Pragmatics* (Cambridge: Cambridge University Press).

Levinson, Stephen (2000) *Presumptive Meanings* (Cambridge, Mass.: MIT Press).

Linsky, Leonard (ed.) (1952) *Semantics and the Philosophy of Language* (Illinois: University of Illinois Press).

Locke, John (1993) *An Essay Concerning Human Understanding* (London: Everyman).

Martin, Robert (1987) *The Meaning of Language* (Cambridge, Mass.: MIT Press).

McCawley, James (1993) *Everything that Linguists have Always Wanted to Know about Logic*, 2nd edn (Chicago, Ill.: University of Chicago Press).

McEnery, Tony and Andrew Wilson (1996) *Corpus Linguistics* (Edinburgh: Edinburgh University Press).

Meyer, Charles (2002) *English Corpus Linguistics* (Cambridge: University of Cambridge Press).

Newmeyer, Frederick (1986) *The Politics of Linguistics* (Chicago, Ill.: University of Chicago Press).

Ochs, Elinor and Bambi Schieffelin (eds) (1979) *Developmental Pragmatics* (New York: Academic Press).

Peirce, C. S. (1992) 'On a new list of categories', in Nathan Houser and Christian Kloesel (eds), *The Essential Peirce, vol. 1* (Bloomington and Indianapolis, Ind.: Indiana University Press) pp. 1–10.

Pinker, Steven (1995) *The Language Instinct* (Harmondsworth: Penguin).

Popper, Karl (2002) *The Logic of Scientific Discovery* (London: Routledge).

Putnam, Hilary (1967) 'The "innateness hypothesis" and explanatory models in linguistics', *Synthesis*, vol. 17, pp. 12–22, reprinted in Ned Block (ed.), *Readings in The Philosophy of Psychology, Vol 2* (London: Methuen, 1981), pp. 292–9.

Quine, W. V. O. (1953) 'Two dogmas of empiricism', in W. V. O. Quine, *From a Logical Point of View* (Cambridge, Mass.: Harvard University Press), pp. 20–4.

Quine, W. V. O. (1960) *Word and Object* (Cambridge, Mass.: MIT Press).

Russell, Bertrand (1905) 'On denoting', *Mind*, vol. 14, pp. 479–93.

Russell, Bertrand (1948) *Human Knowledge: Its Scope and Limits* (London: Allen & Unwin).

Ryle, Gilbert (1963) 'Ordinary language', in Charles Caton (ed.), *Philosophy and Ordinary Language* (Urbana, Ill.: University of Illinois Press), pp. 108–27.

Sampson, Geoffrey (2001) *Empirical Linguistics* (London: Continuum).

Sapir, Edward (1970) *Language* (London: Hart-Davis).

Saussure, Ferdinand de (1960) *Course in General Linguistics*, trans. Wade Baskin (London: Peter Owen).

Savage-Rumbaugh, Sue and Roger Lewin (1994) *Kanzi: The Ape on the Brink of the Human Mind* (New York: John Wiley & Sons).

Schiffer, Stephen (1972) *Meaning* (Oxford: Clarendon Press).

Schiffrin, Deborah (1994) *Approaches to Discourse* (Oxford: Blackwell).

Searle, John (1969) *Speech Acts* (Cambridge: Cambridge University Press).

Searle, John (1979) 'Indirect speech acts', in John Searle, *Expression and Meaning* (Cambridge: Cambridge University Press), pp. 30–57.

Skinner, B. (1957) *Verbal Behavior* (New York: Appleton).

Snow, Catherine (1972) 'Mothers' speech to children learning language', *Child Development*, vol. 43, pp. 549–65.

Snow, Catherine (1977) 'Mothers' speech research: from input to interaction', in Catherine Snow and Charles Ferguson (eds); *Talking to Children* (Cambridge: Cambridge University Press), pp. 31–49.

Snow, Catherine (1986) 'Conversations with children', in Paul Fletcher and Michael Garman (eds), *Language Acquisition*, 2nd edn (Cambridge: Cambridge University Press), pp. 69–89.

Snow, Catherine and Charles Ferguson (eds) (1977) *Talking to Children* (Cambridge: Cambridge University Press).

Sperber, Dan and Deirdre Wilson (1995) *Relevance*, 2nd edn (Oxford: Blackwell).

Spolsky, Bernard (1998) *Sociolinguistics* (Oxford: Oxford University Press).

Stainton, Robert (1996) *Philosophical Perspectives on Language* (Ontario: Broadview).

Strawson, Peter (1950) 'On referring', *Mind, vol.* 59, pp. 320–44.

Strawson, Peter (1964) 'Intention and convention in speech acts', *The Philosophical Review*, vol.73, reprinted in Peter Strawson (1971), *Logico-Linguistic Papers* (London: Methuen), pp. 149–69.

Struhsaker, Thomas T. (1967) 'Auditory communication among vervet monkeys', in Stuart A. Altmann (ed.), *Social Communication among Primates* (Chicago, Ill.: University of Chicago Press), pp. 281–324.

Tarski, Alfred (1944) 'The semantic conception of truth and the foundations of semantics', *Philosophy and Phenomenological Research*, vol. 4, pp. 341–74, reprinted in Leonard Linsky (ed.), *Semantics and the Philosophy of Language* (Illinois: University of Illinois Press, 1952), pp. 13–47.

Terrace, Herbert S. (1980) *Nim* (London: Eyre Methuen).

Von Frisch, K. (1950) *Bees: their Vision, Chemical Sense and Language* (Ithaca, NY: Cornell University Press).

Von Frisch, K. (1954) *The Dancing Bees* (London: Methuen).

Wanner, Eric and Lila Gleitman (eds) (1982) *Language Acquisition: the State of the Art* (Cambridge: Cambridge University Press).

Whorf, Benjamin Lee (1956) *Language, Thought, and Reality* (Cambridge, Mass.: MIT Press).

Index

Lightning Source UK Ltd.
Milton Keynes UK
UKOW06f1325121015

260351UK00010B/320/P